DEEP RIVER TALK

COLLECTED POEMS

HONE TUWHARE

Introduction by Frank Stewart

TALANOA

CONTEMPORARY
PACIFIC
LITERATURE

University of Hawaii Press

Honolulu

To my sons,
Rewi Tamakuru, Andrew, and Robert,
and to their mother, Jean Agnes

First published in New Zealand by Godwit Press Limited 1993
Published in North America by University of Hawaii Press 1994

Printed in the United States of America
94 95 96 97 98 99   5 4 3 2 1

Library of Congress Cataloging-in-Publication Data
Tuwhare, Hone, 1922–
Deep river talk : collected poems / Hone Tuwhare.
p.   cm. — (Talanoa : Contemporary Pacific literature)
Includes index.
ISBN 0–8248–1588–2. — ISBN 0–8248–1607–2 (pbk.)
1. Maori (New Zealand people)—Poetry.   2. New Zealand—Poetry.
I. Title.   II. Series: Talanoa.
PR9639.3.T8A6   1994
821—dc20   93–47103
                                                          CIP

University of Hawaii Press books are printed on acid-free paper
and meet the guidelines for permanence and durability of the
Council on Library Resources

Contents

from *Sapwood and Milk* (1972)

from *Something Nothing* (1974)

from *Making a Fist of It* (1978)

from *Year of the Dog* (1982)

from *Mihi* (1987)

from *Short Back & Sideways* (1992)

New Poems

Editor's Note

Talanoa is proud to publish this collection of poems by Hone Tuwhare, the third book in this series on contemporary Pacific literature.

To *talanoa* is to tell stories to one another. A favorite place for storytelling in the Pacific is around the *kava* bowl, the image of which is the logo of this series. In this communal setting, different voices share their stories. These stories may be funny or sad, fictional or real, ribald or sedate; in short, anything goes in this space of poetic license. Whatever the focus, these stories are rarely boring, for they must capture the attention of the audience and connect with them at an emotional level.

Poetry is the preferred genre of most Pacific writers, its form and rhetorical style reminiscent of the oral literatures of the islands. Standing tall among these writers is Hone Tuwhare, regarded by many as one of New Zealand's best, a true poet who draws from ancestral and European traditions. His is a voice that has been much anthologized in collections of New Zealand poetry for the past sixteen years.

This collection, written over a span of thirty years, speaks in many voices, from different vantage points in time and space, and on a wide range of topics and themes. Through the eyes of the poet, we encounter the physical world of our surroundings and the emotional world within us. In seeing what he saw and feeling what he felt, we can experience our world anew, in its various shades and hues. As we marvel at the clarity of the pictures before us, we are enriched—and sometimes challenged—by the poet's vision.

Some of the reactions of critics and the general public to Tuwhare's poetry are eloquently captured in the accompanying essay by Frank Stewart, author of three books of poetry, professor of English, and editor of several anthologies. Stewart's essay appears at the beginning of this collection, but can be read at any time. Many readers will want to first hear Tuwhare in his own pure voice. If we are open and listen well, we might hear new melodies, undetected by previous ears.

It is now time to *talanoa*. Listen to the poet. Hear him speak to us.

Vilsoni Hereniko

TALANOA
CONTEMPORARY PACIFIC LITERATURE

Vilsoni Hereniko, General Editor

DEEP RIVER TALK

COLLECTED POEMS

Introduction

Desiring to give it high praise, one writer recently called Hone Tuwhare's poetry a "collision" between the language of the working class, the Bible, and Māori *kōrero* (narratives). Another writer, also applauding it, called Tuwhare's poetry "a real mixture . . . as if you're in church and in the pub at the same time."

But the best description of Hone Tuwhare's poems may be that they are not so much a collision of language as the luminous weaving of voices in rich conversation—lyrical talk between the reader and a joyful, exuberant man of many facets and many experiences—a man steeped in the language of the Bible, of Marx and Engels, and of his native New Zealand. A man articulate in the language of love, family, and the world, in a conversation romantic, earthy, funny, and always from the heart.

This conversation comprises not only the many voices of Hone Tuwhare, but the voices of the natural world as well—rain, sea, and sun. On friendly terms, Tuwhare addresses them all, along with a world of sacred objects that listen to and return this talk. In his poems, each part of the world is alive to his language of engagement and rapture. Deep talk, deep river talk.

Hone Tuwhare was born in Kaikohe, in northern New Zealand, in 1922. When he was six years old, his mother died and his father took him to Auckland. There, though the Depression made jobs hard to come by, Hone's father eventually found employment in a Chinese market garden in the suburb of Avondale.

Hone Tuwhare remembers their house being only a tin shack with an earthen floor. But he also remembers his father stressing to him—in a world where extraordinary suffering is all too common—the importance of being grateful for a roof over one's head and proper food to eat. There were fish from the nearby sea and vegetables from the garden, and Tuwhare's father was a good provider. For company, Tuwhare could visit a half-dozen Māori families that lived close by. All in all, life in that small house, embraced closely by his father, seemed, as Tuwhare remembers it—"marvelous."

For the next three years, Tuwhare spoke only the Māori language at home. Afterward, his father would speak only English with him, wanting, like many Māori mothers and fathers, to encourage his son's success at the English-speaking schools.[1] And Tuwhare remembers more encouragement—his father reading to him the English of the King James Bible, and his being taught to read it back aloud.

3

"He used to make me read that, yes," Tuwhare said in a 1988 interview with Bill Manhire.[2] "There's a bit of that kind of structure in some of my poems, you know. A Biblical sort of thing emerges, and I'm sure it's because of that."

The New Testament, especially, got Hone Tuwhare reading and loving English as a young boy. "John in particular," Tuwhare remembers, "because of my name, I suppose: Hone/John. So that was an important thing—the singing cadence and flow, you know, of the Bible when it's read aloud. It must always be read aloud, I reckon."

At the same time, Tuwhare recalls that English was not the only language in his life. After Tuwhare had gone to bed, his father would sometimes stay up at night with a friend and the two men would tell ghost stories to each other in Māori and sing traditional songs. "I'd be listening to them, you know," Tuwhare remembers, "taking it in." And Hone in turn would tell ghost stories to his school friends. "We'd sit there on the footpath and talk away, and then the light would come on. Talk, gosh, and I would be leaning up there against a post, under the light. And I was frightened about walking past the cemetery—where the streetlights cut out before it, you know, and you had to go on through the dark, right down to my place."

Pushed by his father and by his teachers, Tuwhare became a prodigious reader, checking out everything the library had for kids—Hopalong Cassidy, Zane Grey, *Beau Geste, Captain Blood.* And he continued to read the Bible, now the Old Testament—Ecclesiastes, Proverbs, the Song of Solomon—those "beautiful things," he says. "It's bloody good stuff, the Old Testament . . . full of weird, beautiful poetry."

Although he got top marks at school, Tuwhare did not go to college because his father could not afford it. Instead, at age seventeen, he apprenticed at the Railway Workshops at Otahuhu as a boilermaker. "Maybe it's just as well," Tuwhare remembers about missing college. "I probably wouldn't have written any poetry."

By then it was 1939. Within a year the war broke out in the Pacific and Tuwhare tried repeatedly to enlist. Each time he tried, however, he was rejected because of his color blindness. When finally he was accepted, enlisting in the Sixteenth Māori Battalion, the war was winding down and only the occupation of Japan remained. More voices to learn in the army and abroad. More language, more talk.

Before the war was over, Tuwhare had become a fully certified boilermaker, and thus a member of the union; and in the union trade shops he was recruited into the Communist party. The Railway Workshops and the Communist party opened Tuwhare's eyes to politics, to social injustice at home and around the world, and to the problems of working-class people.

"Marxism gave me a real sense of place, you know," Tuwhare remembers. "I had a sense of belonging—being part of a particular class of people." The talk of Marxism and working-class conversation were added to his language.

Then, by joining the Left Book Club library in Darby Street and the union workers' library, Tuwhare found a new literature to feed his love for books: first, a generation of sad and angry American fiction writers sympathetic to social reform, in love with the sound of their own beautiful language, spoken by the poor and the lost—Steinbeck, Hemingway, Dos Passos, Thomas Wolfe—so different from British English. Tuwhare also read the Andalusian poet-martyr Federico García Lorca—"*He* was a bloody good influence!" And for the first time he read the brooding Russian novelists, on fire with God and the loss of God.

But for all the education and sympathy given him by the Communist party, Tuwhare was an independent thinker when it came to politics and justice. When the Russians invaded Hungary in 1956, he resigned from the Party in protest. (He remained out of the Party for nearly twenty years, coming back only in the 1970s to travel to China at the invitation of the People's Republic.)

By 1956 Tuwhare had married Jean McCormack and had started a family. He was working at Mangakino as a tradesman on the hydroelectric project on the Waikato River when, one morning, a policeman came to his door. Tuwhare feared he was going to be arrested for his left-wing organizing. Instead, the officer told him that his father had died. That day he sat down and wrote "Thine Own Hands Have Fashioned," a love poem with a biblical theme. It was his first serious poem. "Very flowery," he says of the poem now, but it opened the well-spring of his writing.

"Thine Own Hands Have Fashioned" was published a year later. And as more of his poems were accepted for publication, Tuwhare gradually began to think of himself as a writer. Seven years later, when Hone was forty-two years old, he published his first book, *No Ordinary Sun* (Auckland: Blackwood and Janet Paul), dedicating it to the memory of his father.

Of this first book of poems, Tuwhare's friend and fellow poet R. A. K. Mason wrote: "Here—and I think this is for the first time—is a member of the Māori race qualifying as a poet in English and in the idiom of his own generation, but still drawing his main strength from his own people. . . . In such a noble poem as 'No Ordinary Sun,' in speaking against atomic evils imperiling our shores, he draws so profoundly from Maoridom that the source can be felt to lie in the depths common to all mankind."

Thirty years later we have Hone Tuwhare's *Deep River Talk*, the collected poems, published outside New Zealand for American readers for the first time. The book contains over 140 poems chosen from Tuwhare's ten volumes of poetry, and it documents the remarkable growth of a gifted Pacific poet over a lifetime of publishing.

The collection is arranged chronologically, beginning with selections from *No Ordinary Sun,* published in 1964. In the first part, the poems are clearly youthful and modest, formal and controlled. Mostly songs, laments, and nocturnes about the sea and the islands, the early lyrics are also about work and dreams; salutes to the sun and to nature. To an American ear, the style at this point is clearly British influenced, which means that the poems echo a high and somewhat elegant verse of an earlier time in England—in contrast to the disruptive, confrontational, and experimental verse being written in America in the 1960s.

But these early poems have wonderful virtues that even a parochial American can hear in the lyrics. They display a youthful joy in the physical world, especially in nature—the rain, the sea, and the sun. And this amazing vitality and optimism stay with Tuwhare throughout his career.

Typical of this section are these romantic, beautifully cadenced lines from "Roads":

I have learned to love
too much perhaps
rough tracks hard of going
poorly lit by stars.

Beneath his tender romanticism, however, Tuwhare sounds his despair at the displacement of the sacred natural world by modern industrialization. In "The Sea, to the Mountains, to the River" he writes,

Here
alien sounds are struck.
Nowhere is there greater fuss
to tear out the river's tongue.

Blue hiss and crackle
of the welding rod,
compressed sigh of air
and the whump and whoof
fuse to the rising clamour
of the rivet gun.

In poems from Tuwhare's second and third volumes, *Come Rain Hail* and *Sapwood and Milk,* his empathy with nature remains, expressed in poems addressed to natural objects and phenomena. And he increases his use of two other forms of subject matter: the first is Māori myth and local color; and the second is contemporary politics, rendered in a sturdy vernacular.

The stronger presence of Māori myth and local color is exemplified best in the opening lines of "Tangi-Hanga" where the poet says,

> Rest, Matiu. Lie easy
> My voice grown tall has found legs
>
> *I sense your apprehension: know*
> *that your canoe teeters*
> *on inconclusive reefs of argument*

Tuwhare often turns to the Māori tradition of formal lamentation—a *waiata-tangi* is a song of lament, a *tangi-hanga* is a wake—writing poems of death and loss, the counter pole as always to a poet's love for the living and for life.

The importance to Tuwhare of accurately portraying home and community is evident in such poems as "Village in Savaii: Western Samoa," in which he says,

> God, I need something more than the Gauguin
> clichés of mysterious, heavy-limbed
> unsmiling women.

Tuwhare's social consciousness, often expressed in the vernacular, also receives renewed emphasis in the early 1970s. The best example of this is "Martin Luther King," a poem on the civil rights leader's assassination. In it Tuwhare declares, "When you slumped down, mankind / was hurled back a billion years, to a / jellyfish." And he ends the poem with a self-conscious recognition of his own obligation to speak out in poetry on issues of justice:

> Before your light was snuffed out, you asked
> for a song sung real sweet: hell,
> this ain't much. Treacle in my veins: death-cart
> rumble in my ears.

This anger mixed with obligation, which has joined rather than replaced the romanticism of Tuwhare's first volume, appears in such poems as "To a Maori figure cast in bronze outside the Chief Post Office, Auckland." Here, as in many of his poems, he is affronted by injustice and his preferred form of protest is satire and disrespectful wit.

The overly formal elegance of the early work has faded by Tuwhare's third book. Despite the added subject matter and more informal language, however, he is still in many ways a poet of love. We can see this love and his expanded range of influences—including poetry by Americans—in the poem "Sandra," with its earnest, colloquial cadences. The lyric ends:

> Girl, I can't write a pretty poem
> for your thirteenth birthday.
> I write only to thank you for the
> plate of marinaded fish-flesh
> which awakened my taste-buds
> yesterday:
>
> and to tell you tonight
> of the furl of music unfolding
> to the wind's swirl on the cypress
> tree next door: imperious rap
> of rain on the windows.

By Tuwhare's fourth and fifth books, *Something Nothing* and *Making a Fist of It*, published in the late 1970s, he is a fully confident poet with his own style and a clear, engaging voice. He continues to expand his subject matter; he visits China, for example, and comments on international politics. At the same time, he finds a way to incorporate Māori words and phrases into his English-language poems in a manner that is wholly natural and elegant. He uses humor more often—for its satiric and witty effect, as before, but now also for its own sake.

Still, as much as Tuwhare is now humorous, he is frequently outraged—his strongest and most striking political statements come in the poem "Making a fist of it," which concerns the Soweto riots, and in "Rain-maker's song for Whina," about the overland march by Māori in the mid-1970s to protest the loss of their land. He continues to strive for poetic language and form of the highest kind. And he continues to be a poet of love and the natural world.

Tuwhare's volumes from the 1980s are no less strong than the earlier work. In fact, some of his best poems to date come in *Year of the Dog*, published in 1982. They include "Status-seeker" and "The river is an island," both full of exuberance and energy, shifting between formality and informality, wit and sincerity, Māori language and high and low English.

In the 1980s Tuwhare visited Europe and expanded his range of subjects even more. At the same time, his connection to home never diminished and, if anything, grew stronger in his poetry. In the selections from his 1987 book, *Mihi*, we see the second poem in *Deep River Talk* written entirely in the Māori language. (The first, "He waiata whaka-honore atu ki a Haki raua ko Hohepa," appeared in *Year of the Dog*.)

The selections from the 1992 book *Short Back & Sideways* and the work in the final section, called *New Poems*, are as entertaining and strongly crafted as the poetry in any of the previous sections. Though seventy years of age by this time, Tuwhare illuminates the page with the same energy and skill he had as a younger poet—and the same extraordinary weaving of voices. The poems range from "Sun o (2)," written in dialect and beginning,

> Gissa smile sun, giss yr best
> good mawnin' one, fresh 'n cool like
>
> yore still comin' — still
> half in an' half outa the lan'scape?

to "He pao reka mo Huaonia," written entirely in Māori. And the subject matter continues to be equally wide ranging, from comments on political subjects and international settings to lyrical poems of nature and human companionship, the sincere poems of rapture.

When asked recently his ideas about how an artist works, Tuwhare said, "Most art, I think, is in praise of something. It might be a dynasty, it might be a tribe, it might be a person. You know, you write a love poem to someone; you paint someone whom you love. You carve something. . . . but basically I think art is intended to please, to praise, to highlight."

The heart displayed in this answer identifies Hone Tuwhare as a true poet. Without overlooking the causes that need fighting and the wrongs that need correcting, he is able to love and admire, from which understanding nearly always tends to follow.

Possessed by a passion for the natural world and for community, Tuwhare deserves to be read by all who love language and life—the talk and the river—deep river talk.

Frank Stewart

Notes

1. A written form of the Māori language has existed since 1815, but its use, along with the use of spoken Māori, was severely discouraged by the early English-speaking immigrants who colonized the land. Beginning in 1867, schools in New Zealand were conducted only in English, and by the 1970s just 2 percent of Māori children were speaking Māori as their first language. Not until 1987 did an act of parliament declare Māori an official language of New Zealand and establish a commission to promote its revitalization.

2. Most of Hone Tuwhare's quotations here are from Bill Manhire's interview with the poet, titled "Ready to Move," *Landfall* 167 (1988). Others are from "Thine own hand, mate," in Greg O'Brien and Robert Cross, *Moments of Invention: Portraits of 21 New Zealand Writers* (Auckland: Heinemann Reed, 1988).

from

NO ORDINARY SUN

Time and the child

Tree earth and sky
reel to the noontide beat
of sun and the old man
hobbling down the road.
Cadence —

of sun-drowned cicada
in a child's voice shrilling:
. . . are you going man?

Where are going man where —
The old man is deaf
to the child.
His stick makes deep
holes in the ground.
His eyes burn to a distant point

where all roads converge . . .
The child has left his toys
and hobbles after the old
man calling: funny man funny man

funny old man funny
Overhead the sun paces
and buds pop and flare.

That morning early

Started up that morning
to stomach pinch and growls: listened
to the sound of hail nick on glass
and iron roof.

Heard the rain applauding: the lilt
and swell fading to the wind's flirt
over the gaunt flank of the land

and wondered

how long it would be
before Nanny with her brown dimpled skin
and goat-nanny smell would come
bearing leaves of koromiko
and black cauldron aswirl
with the mangled roots of flax or lawyer vine
to chide and O most firmly to assure me
that all my rumble belly yearnings shall match
the fearful splendour of riven skies
mending . . .

Woke up that long-away morning
to stomach pinch nipping
and a lip-locked moan escaping

Roads

I turn away from roads,
sign-posted hot macadams:
roads on smooth roads curving
looping under, up and yonder
going leading nowhere.

I dream of roads
but seek instead a tumble
stumble-footed course I know
will earn me sad wounds
cutting deep to bone.

I have learned to love
too much perhaps
rough tracks hard of going
poorly lit by stars.

Night-long voyagings
have found no easy path
to the silent gate
that is the dawn —
the truth beyond
that is the banished city.

Hearing only the night-birds
booming ancient blasphemies:
moon-dark ease reflection
in the knocking stones
the river chortling.

Song

Gay wind
impudent lover of trees
why do you sing grey lamentations
to a sallow sky?

The headlands await your coming
and the mute crags lend a pensive
ear to the listless drag of the sea's feet.

Tree
your muscles leap and tense
but will not free the wind
held captive in your branches.

Gay wind
why do you sing grey lamentations
to a sallow sky?

Nocturne

And if the earth should tremble
to the sea's unfathomed rage
it is because the sun has fled
uncupping the stone nipples
of the land.

The moon has torn
from the pulsing arm of the sea
a tawdry bracelet . . . and I
alone am left
with the abandoned earth
the night-sea sobbing.

My heart shall limping come
to police the night
so that no surly light
shall flare
nor sad spring blood forth
a despondent moon
to limn the swollen night
in anguish.

The sea, to the mountains, to the river

Far off
the sea beckons
to the mountains.

Austerely
the mountains ponder
the cacophonic river tossing
white-splintered mane to the
mist's swirl.

Here
alien sounds are struck.
Nowhere is there greater fuss
to tear out the river's tongue.

Blue hiss and crackle
of the welding rod,
compressed sigh of air
and the whump and whoof
fuse to the rising clamour
of the rivet gun.

Cursing
scuffing the earth with massive
boots, men are walking away:
and from a smoke-wreathed shoulder
of a crouching hill a gigantic fist
of sound unfolds — shattering the clouds.

Coaxed into staccato life
a tractor nonchalantly puffs
perfect rings into the startled air.

Exulting men
as skilled as spiders thread
a skyline of steel crucifixes.

The sea beckons
again and again
to the mountains. Unmoved
the austere mountains ponder
a silence as profound as stars.

Burial

In a splendid sheath
of polished wood and glass
with shiny appurtenances
lay he fitly blue-knuckled
and serene:

hurry rain and trail him
to the bottom of the grave

Flowers beyond budding
will not soften the gavel's
beat of solemn words
and hard sod thudding:

hurry rain and seek him
at the bottom of the grave

Through a broken window
inanely looks he up;
his face glass-gouged and bloodless
his mouth engorging clay
for all the world uncaring . . .

Cover him quickly, earth!
Let the inexorable seep of rain
finger his greening bones, deftly.

Lament (1)

In that strident summer of battle
    when cannon grape and ball
    tore down the pointed walls
    and women snarled as men
    and blood boiled in the eyes:
    in the proud winter of defeat
    he stood unweary
    and a god among men.

He it was whom death looked hotly on
    whilst I in adoration
    brought timid fuel to his fire:
    of all things manly he partook

Yet did it plummet down like a bird
    engulfing him as he headlong
    rushed towards the night,
    the long night
    where no dawn wakes to pale
    the quaking stars: farewell

Farewell companion of laughter and light
    who warmed the nights with the
    croaking chants of olden times: hear
    me now sing poorly sing harshly . . .

At dawn's light I looked for you
    at land's end where two oceans froth
    but you had gone without leaving a sign
    or a whispered message to the gnarled
    tree's feet or the grass or the inscrutable
    rock face. Even the innocent day-dreaming
    moon could not explain the wind's wry mirth.

To you it seems I am nothing —
    a nobody and of little worth
    whom the disdainful years
    neither praise nor decry
    but shall abandon to fat
    and the vast delight of worms: farewell

Farewell farewell
    Let the heavens mumble and stutter
    Let them acknowledge your leaving us
    Mine is the lone gull's cry in the night
    Let my grief hide the moon's face
    Let alien gods salute thee and
    with flashing knives cut open
    the dark belly of the sky.

I feel rain spit in my face

I bear no malice, let none stain my valedictions
For I am at one with the wind
the clouds' heave and the slapping rain
the tattered sky the wild solitude
of the sea and the streaming earth
which I kneel to kiss . . .

This poem was suggested by a tangi in Sir George Grey's *Nga Motcatca*.

21

Tangi

I did not meet her
on the bordered path
nor detect her fragrance
in the frolic of violets
and carnations.

She did not stroll riverward
to sun-splash and shadows
to willows trailing garlands
of green pathos.

Death was not hiding in the cold rags
of a broken dirge:
nor could I find her
in the cruel laughter of children,
the curdled whimper of a dog.

But I heard her with the wind
crooning in the hung wires
and caught her beauty by the coffin
muted to a softer pain —
in the calm vigil of hands
in the green-leaved anguish
of the bowed heads
of old women.

The old place

No one comes
by way of the doughy track
through straggly tea tree bush
and gorse, past the hidden spring
and bitter cress.

Under the chill moon's light
no one cares to look upon
the drunken fence-posts
and the gate white with moss.

No one except the wind
saw the old place
make her final curtsy
to the sky and earth:

and in no protesting sense
did iron and barbed wire
ease to the rust's invasion
nor twang more tautly
to the wind's slap and scream.

On the cream-lorry
or morning paper van no one comes,
for no one will ever leave
the golden city on the fussy train;
and there will be no more waiting
on the hill beside the quiet tree
where the old place falters
because no one comes any more

no one.

Friend

Do you remember
that wild stretch of land
with the lone tree guarding the point
from the sharp-tongued sea?

The fort we build out of branches
wrenched from the tree is dead wood now.
The air that was thick with the whirr of
toetoe spears succumbs at last to the grey gull's wheel.

Oyster-studded roots
of the mangrove yield no finer feast
of silver-bellied eels, and sea-snails
cooked in a rusty can.

Allow me to mend the broken ends
of shared days:
but I wanted to say
that the tree we climbed
that gave food and drink
to youthful dreams, is no more.
Pursed to the lips her fine-edged
leaves made whistle — now stamp
no silken tracery on the cracked
clay floor.

Friend,
in this drear
dreamless time I clasp
your hand if only to reassure
that all our jewelled fantasies were
real and wore splendid rags.

Perhaps the tree
will strike fresh roots again:
give soothing shade to a hurt and
troubled world.

Not by wind ravaged

Deep scarred
　　not by wind ravaged nor rain
　　nor the brawling stream:
　　stripped of all save the brief finery
　　of gorse and broom; and standing
　　sentinel to your bleak loneliness
　　the tussock grass —

Of voiceless land, let me echo your desolation.
　　The mana of my house has fled,
　　the marae is but a paddock of thistle.
　　I come to you with a bitterness
　　that only your dull folds can soothe
　　for I know, I know
　　my melancholy chants shall be lost
　　to the wind's shriek about the rotting eaves.

Distribute my nakedness —
　　Unadorned I come with no priceless
　　offering of jade and bone curio: yet
　　to the wild berry shall I give
　　a tart piquancy; enhance for a deathless
　　space the fragile blush of manuka . . .

You shall bear all and not heed.
　　In your huge compassion embrace
　　those who know no feeling other
　　than greed:
　　of this I lament my satisfaction
　　for it is as full as a beggar's cup:
　　no less shall the dust of avaricious men
　　succour exquisite blooms with
　　moist lips parting
　　to the morning sun.

Mauri

Ere gods were shaped
to polished images of brass
and fired clay
the meek stone hardened
to a consciousness its own.

From its soul's core, sun
to another sun responded:
succoured the lonely man
his tribe's invention of trees
sweeping the sky's floor clean.

When gods were fused
to an angered one
all-seeing triple-faced
still
did this man's tribe store
reverence for the stone
from where plants sprang
sweet water leapt:

and jealous of its wellspring
destroyed utterly
the new god's sour
and honeyed strength
turning alas
the meek stone's joy
to a cloud
to an ashen face.

Mauri is a material symbol of the hidden principle protecting vitality.
Life principle, talisman, thymos of man. (Denotative meaning taken from
Dictionary of Maori Language compiled by the Rev. Hoani Laughton.)

A disciple dreams

I walked with him —
and when he spoke my eyes
opened to strange happenings
and I looked down into the gasping mouths
of fishes with eyes like round
black bread and tails quivering as
silvered wine that had not been darkened
by his blood . . .

Yet did I see him squinting at the sky
in the manner of men
born to the sea:
and I knew a deep dread for I saw
a wrathful army on black steeds, massing.

Miraculous how my fears were laid:
and calmly did he bid us all
to eat of the blessed food
and straightway knelt we down
to partake of his bounty.

And so it was that in the midst of feasting
and thanksgiving the storm fell upon us
with a fury that no one could quell: the wind tore
futile protestations from his lips
and the seas threshed
and lightning shattered the loaves
and little fishes
and the heavens spat venom on the faces
of those whose meatless arms were thin armour
to the pitiless rain:
my rage grew to the topmost wave —
and I awoke engulfed in tears:
my fists beating the floor of my
stone room.

No ordinary sun

Tree let your arms fall:
raise them not sharply in supplication
to the bright enhaloed cloud.
Let your arms lack toughness and
resilience for this is no mere axe
to blunt nor fire to smother.

Your sap shall not rise again
to the moon's pull.
No more incline a deferential head
to the wind's talk, or stir
to the tickle of coursing rain.

Your former shagginess shall not be
wreathed with the delightful flight
of birds nor shield
nor cool the ardour of unheeding
lovers from the monstrous sun.

Tree let your naked arms fall
nor extend vain entreaties to the radiant ball.
This is no gallant monsoon's flash,
no dashing trade wind's blast.
The fading green of your magic
emanations shall not make pure again
these polluted skies . . . for this
is no ordinary sun.

O tree
in the shadowless mountains
the white plains and
the drab sea floor
your end at last is written.

Never look back

The years replete with love
    and the fattening of one's self
    have all but slain the memory
    hot white-knuckled outbursts of old.

    About those days I care no more.
    Hail it only as the turning point
    in Time and yet disown
    Time's standing and her own.

Tastes were sharper then;
    sandwich spread was dripping fat
    on a dry old crust
    saliva'd exaltation
    to heaven's doorstep pure
    and juicy angels.

Slack and famine-eyed
    myself did see myself
    in other wretches' eyes
    statureless, undignified.
    No thing fanciful nor ghosts
    but O too real and thin
    and blessed hot the soup
    from Salvation's army-kitchen.

Of those lean days
    I cannot rouse myself to rave
    with equal heat
    nor filch from Time a morsel
    of hard wisdom
    knowing already and too late
    Time's answer shall be final,
    sure, and just.

Moon daughter

And all your sobbing hurt
and frustrate womb through
pensive days shall run to quench
your eager fire.

No impious wind violate
your doubtful ease
nor yet shall tender rain glad
tidings bring to sharpen old desires
for the sun and flowers
till burning nights turn flaccid
all the pale moon's growth
and menses.

Daughter, daughter
know you soon enough
virgin nipples harden
to a sly man's touch.

The girl in the park

The girl in the park
    saw a nonchalant sky
    shrug into a blue-dark
    denim coat.

    The girl in the park
    did not reach up to touch
    the cold steel buttons.

The girl in the park
    saw the moon glide into a dead tree's arms
    and felt the vast night
    pressing.
    How huge it seems,
    and the trees are big, she said.

    The stars heard her
    and swooped down perching
    on treetop and branch
    owl-like and unblinking.

The grave trees,
    as muscular as her lover
    leaned darkly down to catch
    the moonrise and madness
    in her eyes:
    the moon is big, it is very big,
    she said, with velvet in her throat.

    An owl hooted.
    The trees scraped and nudged
    each other and the stars
    carried the helpless
    one-ribbed moon away . . .

The girl in the park
    does not care: her body swaying
    to the dark-edged chant
    of storms.

Importune the east wind

East Wind
do not rage your brothers
to a harsh awakening.
Hush me
to a Tuesday's blossoming tree
and the wild orchard
where I shall find her.

Gentle her to sow
unto the dumb heart's field
words more lovely
than I have ever gleaned from stones
as red as nectarines.

Morning of Tuesday bring
hand-clasps and wonderment
at the sun's appearing.
And mine be that day
to greet as eagerly:

so that she may lift closed eyes,
and nose as delicately the salt
of your coming
that was lately of the sea, the sea's groan,
and the festooned rocks, o East Wind.

Sea call

Let the radio pip and shudder
at each dawn's news

Let the weatherman hint
a gaunt meaning to the chill
and ache of bone:
but when the new moon's bowl
is storing rain, the pull of time
and sea will cry to me
again.

And I shall stuff my longing
in an empty pack
and hasten to the secret shore
where the land's curve lies
clad in vermilion — and the green
wind tugging gravely.

There let the waves lave
pleasuring the body's senses,
and the sun's feet
shall twinkle and flex
to the sea-egg's needling
and the paua's stout kiss
shall drain a rock's heart
to the sandbar's booming.

Thine own hands have fashioned

(poem for male and female voice)

O let the vain sun die
with a peacock flourish
so that I may rise from
my labours and hasten
to light up the dark tent
that is . . . Delilah

Beloved
      thine hands are distraught winds
      waking the dead cymbalic reeds
      at the edge of the lake.
      Hear ye the sullen moan of
      yielding trees
      the forlorn sighs of tormented hills
      the liquid gasp of molten valleys.

At your coming
      the surface of the moonless lake
      stiffens . . .

Beloved
      thine hands tongue an unalien speech
      with a maddening reticence:
      thine ostrich hands my lord
      are insultingly deaf to the pulsing
      clangour of the blood
      and the urgent bell.
      Rend them!
      Destroy thy belltower of love.
      Plunder thy storehouse of spices.

My lord
      thine hands drop with golden flowers
      from the lion's maw:
      thine hands contain the splendid fire
      of poised lances:
      they are exquisite pinnacles
      of light O lord . . .

34

Hear me
    I beseech thee
    when eagle screams fly up
    and a thousand gleaming spears
    impale the skies
    in the mounting savagery and
    the lull . . .

My lord my love
    . . . your hands are beautiful

Prelude?

Suddenly
he felt tired:
lay down
and died.

Shared no regrets:
his soul freed
from a broken shell
stepped sprightly
as a new-born chick:

Gave no heed
nor feather turned
to the shocked cry
heart-wails
the shattered teacup
and milk
spilling on the floor.

Where shall I wander

People leave I know
for therapeutic purposes
and sometimes for no reason
some leave anyway to war
for another job to go somewhere
anywhere
but it's not of these I talk
some are forced to leave

and of these
I can think of reasons
circumstantial turning luck
to bad bad because
in each case others
glad to see the back of them make
farewell speeches full
of cheap regrets to drive them
far away

Best not to leave a mark
behind for good or ill
indifference then would rule no song
or dance disgruntled shouts
bands come out to play

Terminals railway stations
aren't people's palaces exactly
poor-lit waiting rooms stewed
tea and buns and echoing as mournful
duet-farewell
of train and chained dog howling
to the clack of the wheels
in the head

Old man chanting in the dark

Where are the men of mettle?
    are there old scores
    left to settle?
    when will the canoes leap
    to the stab and kick
    the sea-wet flourish
    of pointed paddles?
    will the sun play again
    to the skip of muscles
    on curved backs bared
    to the rain's lash
    the sea's punch?
    to War! to War!

where are the proud lands
    to subdue — and women?
    where are the slaves
    to gather wood for the fires
    stones for the oven?
    who shall reap
    the succulent children whimpering
    on the terraced hill-top?

no more alas no more
    no raw memory left
    of these
    nor bloody trophies:
    only the fantail's flip
    to cheeky war-like postures
    and on the sand-hill
    wry wind fluting
    the bleached bones marrowless

Muscle and bone of song

And of trees and the river
no more say
that these alone are sources
for the deft song and the sad:
nor from wave-curl and the sun
cross moon wind and hail
calm and storm come.

Joyously I sing
to the young girl's hip-knock
and taunt: swing-cheerful breasts
shape my hands
to eternal begging-bowls.

Wai-o-Rore (Te Kaha)

Corrugated rust-smitten
cook and eating place
doorless lean-away earth closet
at Wai-o-Rore.

Peach tree and fig
walnut plum and apple
in their wild season
burgeon here.

Toihau (clan meeting-house)
seaward pops an eye
at Whakaari
Whakaari with her white-puffed
thighs outspread.

At Wai-o-Rore Wai-o-Rore
a dying macrocarpa shreds
the wind to flax: two nights
running heard creek-swell
and thump of rain: sea
shouting endless imprecations
to the land.

When pohutukawa bleed
their short-lived brilliance
yellow-fat and full
the kina are at Wai-o-Rore:
where the sluiced black rocks
define the blondness
of splintered wave: sun
whip mild and gentle.

Whakaari: White Island, Bay of Plenty.

Rain-talk and fever

Menacingly, and above your thrumming
that strange malady sidewise squirming;
surfacing, to make a sharp stir.

And you rain, raining there, outside,
incessantly,
(O, and with such a long night to appease.)

At last, the fever's arched back snapping;
peace, with a cool hand sitting on the bed:
beautiful. And suddenly

you were no longer there. Your sooth-sayer
voice in commiseration had vanished.
But how timely and reassuring to hear

the clock jangling the sure hour before
dawn. Ah rain, I can barely remember
the coiled and stubborn malady you helped

to float to a high dry place.
Quietened now, and like a derelict cat
cleaning itself.

A burnt offering to your greenstone eyes, Tangaroa

When I go, Earth, I shall not succumb
to your pervasive clutch:

nor forbear the sun's hot licks,
or ribbed umbrella of rain slanting.

I'll not crouch there to the lee side;
sit lonely in the shadow of the wind.

Burnt and sere, my soul on ashen wings
shall dust instead the leaning

greenstone walls of Tangaroa advancing,
crumbling . . .

*Ah, then watch him froth and gag, Earth.
Watch him heave!*

Tangaroa: the ocean god

from

COME RAIN HAIL

Haiku (1)

Stop
your snivelling
creek-bed:

come rain hail
and flood-water

laugh again

Rain

I can hear you
making small holes
in the silence
rain

If I were deaf
the pores of my skin
would open to you
and shut

And I
should know you
by the lick of you
if I were blind

the something
special smell of you
when the sun cakes
the ground

the steady
drum-roll sound
you make
when the wind drops

But if I
should not hear
smell or feel or see
you

you would still
define me
disperse me
wash over me
rain

Flood

In the back country
hard rain
is bucketing

Here
in the narrowing light
the river bellows
fatly

From high ground
I mark
twin rows of willow
dishevelled arms
clutching drunk roots
hoarding
bits of old bridge-planking
the body of a beast
puff-bellied
hind feet sticking out

I ask:
when will the waters clear
the eels breathe easy again?

Shall I be able to ford
the river soon: visit
a lean Aunt?

Drunk

When they hustled him out
at closing time he had
forty cents clutched in
his hands for another drink

Rain stabbed the streets
with long slivers of light
He picked his way
gingerly treading the golden
non-existent stairs
to the fried-fish shop

Whirling pinpoints
of coloured lights confused
him: and when people appeared
to converge on him he swerved
to avoid them and collided
with a post

He sensed a sea of receding
faces picked himself up
and promptly emptied his guts
on the footpath fervently calling
for his bleeding mate Christ
who was nowhere to be seen

Later wearing a stiff mask
of indifference
he pissed himself in the bus

At work the next morning
he moved with effort in the hollow
silence of a self-built tomb:
unaware of the trapped mortal
crouching there

Song to a swinging contemplative: Dunedin

Yesterday when she came
a smile dimpled her glasses
She looked out of the tall windows
to the broken quarry face: sensed
the traffic-knock below the trees'
first green breath stirring
And turning to me with the composure
of a Queen Penguin said: You must
leave these buildings. They're unhealthy

On a four-wheeled chariot rode
with her to the Rock at St Kilda:
to the headland where a geyser played
the ninth wave. Long kelp strands swirling
a baptismal of green-haired daughters:
slow indrawn sea-snore grind of teeth

Later at the Cathedral heart-sway
as gentle as a bell afraid to dong:
caught up in a curtsying flurry
of hand-crossed water: coloured glass
filtering a late sun

And passing the slow Stations wondered
when we should reach the painted Lady
before whom I heard my Sister say: I do not
like these plaster-cast Virgins —

For chrissake (under my breath)
You're hard to please.
What do you want, Michelangelo's 'Pieta'?

But yes she said turning
to watch the children and quiet priests
come separately in to lip
the brine of His sad wounds
the vinegar in the blood
the rough dry bread of love

The sport

He died suddenly
a week before the Winter Cup Race
His sporting friends at least
would have no difficulty
in remembering the date

At his home he was arranged neatly
on makeshift flower-decked bier
A steady stream of relatives
and friends came to inspect him:
he was well liked

On the third day a fly buzzed him
but nothing miraculous occurred
Later a special box arrived in which
he was placed and hermetically sealed
A piece of glass
set into the lid above his face
enabled people to view him
without curling their nostrils
fastidiously

A man of substance
it was said of him. Not showy mind.
Took a bus occasionally. Gave generously
to Church and the Intellectually
Handicapped: owned a string of racehorses
and a mistress

When he was buried rain held off
until the last clot of earth
had been patted down
When rain fell jubilation ran high among
those who knew that his horses performed
rather well on a heavy track

He was a good punter

Hotere

When you offer only three
vertical lines precisely drawn
and set into a dark pool of lacquer
it is a visual kind of starvation:

and even though my eyeballs
roll up and over to peer inside
myself, when I reach the beginning
of your eternity I say instead: hell
let's have another feed of mussels

Like, I have to think about it, man

When you stack horizontal lines
into vertical columns which appear
to advance, recede, shimmer and wave
like exploding packs of cards
I merely grunt and say: well, if it
is not a famine, it's a feast

I have to roll another smoke, man

But when you score a superb orange
circle on a purple thought-base
I shake my head and say: hell, what
is this thing called *aroha*

Like, I'm euchred, man. I'm eclipsed?

Tangi-hanga

Rest, Matiu. Lie easy
My voice grown tall has found legs

I sense your apprehension: know
that your canoe teeters
on inconclusive reefs of argument

I will beach your canoe
For I am your mother's kin
and she is my sister who before her
death wished only that her body
be returned to her people and lands
to the south: rest easy

I too have listened to the interminable
noise: an abomination of mock-lily
concern: my buttocks numbed beyond care
or art by arrogant speeches of welcome

Though my words to you are gentle
my brow is lined and crossed with anger

Northern blood of Matiu
hear me without preliminary
Your loud-mouthed declamations resolve
nothing

Observe: his ears are red and stuffed
sore with your bickerings
Together you've blinked the owls to sleep
the sea to embarrassed mutterings
A turd upon you all. On your collective
ignorance may the cunt of Hine-nui-te-po*
squint a baleful eyeball before pissing

Agh! My thoughts gather in my mouth
like soured spittle: I claim Matiu

52

For tomorrow before the sun at noon can cast
fresh shadows on the road we shall have
shaken the dust from this place: this place
where more value is placed on the material
substance he leaves behind than the memory
of his pulse and heart for men

It is finished: I turn away

*Hine-nui-te-po is the death goddess, whom the impudent demi-god Maui
tried to conquer by entering her womb while asleep. At this sight the fantail
could not contain itself and laughed, waking the goddess, who clenched her
thighs and strangled Maui.

At a tangi-hanga it is customary to address the dead person first, as if still
alive, and where appropriate to claim kinship. Often the speaker then publicly
and dramatically asserts a prior right to take the body for burial to his own
tribal grounds. This claim may not be valid, being often challenged; its aim is
to share the burden of grief and flatter the close relatives of the deceased.

Deliver us . . .

They speak in tight
esoteric voices:

a special monkey-language
superbly designed to
conceal
the very secret very
complex technological
know-how
of cracking nuts

Monkey-wise
a mental finger game
wholly absorbing
but which tends to reduce
a mountain
to a dunghill

Meantime
the dull excommunicants
go on cracking
the tougher nuts merely
by bashing them with
bigger rocks

Who tests today?

Something stirs in the night
A cat? A fish? A rat?
How strange. Am I dreaming?
Rain-pimples on glass: are they real?
Is the door unhinged?

It is not a cat. It is not a fish
Neither rat   door-bang   nor trickle
of rain on the windows

It is the void: the stillness in the void
emptied of all sound. There is no human cry
glad or sad: cat-spit   fish-burp   rat-squeal

The door you see has quite effaced itself
and is at one with the molten glass
and hinge
The houses are as powder   sweet smelling
talcum-dust: there is nothing

And the stillness? Ah yes
The stillness may I say is Absolute
The Ascension is complete: and the people
long gone to Christ knows where
with a whopping great hallelujah shout: this

is no dream
Something stirs in the night
A cat-fish-rat? A door slammed shut?
And the rain? What of the rain?

It is silent. It is insidious
It falls: there is no comment

Child coming home in the rain from the store

for Lisa

When I see you pause
make talk dawdle-walk
on the back road to your house
your house overlooking
the timber mill and timber yard
I know you stop only to talk
not to the cruel metalled road
but to a stone   a solitary stone
sharp-edged with flat shiny
faces

Through your mind's eye know
the feel of washed leaves
made green again: tall rain-shafts
drifting: wind wincing
a water-filled pothole

And I child-delighting share
your long walk your talk
to things   *and for things* along
the bent road where impatiently
others wait for the damp bread
you bring

Prodigal City

I walked the City last night
stopping to take everything in:
walking on again in the rain

In the rain in sandals
wet feet slip-slopping: I didn't mind
barely hearing the whine and throb
of trolley bus

wriggling my squeegee toes to gawp
at the mill and swirl of people
multi-coloured and lit up like birthday
candles

And the City seemed
the same lovely woman I used to know
grown somewhat more ample more assured
with new baubles on display

So this is you I said embracing her: you
are wearing well
You don't look too bad yourself she said:
how about some jazz?
I'll have some of that I said

Come then: in this cellar the music
is clipped and punctual
warm and pulsing underneath she said
clicking her fingers

And my feet slip-slopped as I walked the
City last night with the rain on my raincoat
tapping

from

SAPWOOD AND MILK

Wind song and rain

A poem is
a ripple of words
on water wind-huffed

But still water
is a poem winded: a
mirrored distortion
of sky
and mountain
trees and a drowned

face waiting
for a second wind
(a second coming?)
rain
oblivion

Ripple of words
on water

Study in black and white

A friend rang me last week as soon as he got
back from the Antarctic. Wonderful wonderful:
he seemed genuinely pleased to find me in
but in a careful voice asked if I could look
after something for him. I know,
you've brought back a lump of coal, I said.

I have a King Penguin in my fridge.
I look in on it every day as it stands there
with a huge egg between its feet, waiting . . .
Stolid, taciturn, it shares the fish with the
cat, the raw minced meat with me.
It stands there with its head absolutely still.
Only its eyes follow me when they are not
already glazed in sleep: I've grown fond of it.

And I'm not the only one.
In this house people come together mainly to
say true and surprising things about each other.
The light-hearted irreverent ones unhappily
have turned particularly grave; frequently
begging me to open the fridge door.
Wonderful, they chant, stroking it: truly wonderful.
I hate it when they go on like that.
Any moment now I'm afraid, they will deify it.

I should ring my friend
to ask if there is a ship or plane leaving soon
for the Antarctic: because I really think
King Penguin would be happier standing shoulder to
shoulder with his Royal brothers, each with an egg
at its feet, their backs to the wind and driven
snow, waiting:
for the F.A. Cup winners with the colourful jerseys
red noses, flapping arms, to trot on to the
snow-field in single file.

King Penguins should all kick off then and watch the visitors
really break up in a beautiful shower of soaring
eggshells and baby penguins wonderful wonderful.

In October,
Mary quite contemporary
will be seven months gone

Today she walks with the sun
friendly by her side
faking a coarse delight in
throwing a bulbous shadow on
a concrete wall

Obsequiously, the wind retreats
before the shifting surface
of polka dots and bumps that is
her spinnaker-dress

Sun-wreathed, her face quirks
a Mona Lisa: for tomorrow
her plump majesty shall wear
a crown of pain to His coming

Litany

And he
made them
male and female
as a likeness
unto himself

A faceless
hermaphrodite:
in turn
displaying
much lovingness
much sternness
too much hair

And on
the outside
of the outside walls
fisting the air:
a flabbergast
of sinner
sensualist
unbeliever: pray

may it always be

Sapwood and milk

I should not have known you
were it not for bowers
indecorously fashioned to such
coarse bowing and trampling
subtle belling of leaves
squinch of grass. And in the

lilt and mesh of eyes
golden slices of the peach-moon's
merriment

Village in Savaii: Western Samoa

In the shade of the store verandah
    women sit hunched cross-legged
    checking the day's total of gossip.
    They've lost one because there's a hell
    of a search going on: tremors of laughter.
    They stop fanning themselves when I
    unhitch the camera.

    But my eye has caught the naked
    two-year-old soft-flopping around on
    the white expanse of concrete where cocoa
    beans dry in the sun. His mountain grandmother
    shuffles over: her hands stretched out to him.
    Leai: I shake my head at her. She nods and
    backs out of the frame: I wait.

    Unaided the child climbs to his feet.
    Cocoa beans are imbedded in his buttocks.

From a side door I hear you call me: surprised.
    When I try to set you up you say, Leai: and
    disappear.
    Leai: lay me: lay you: Ioe! Girl, I only want
    to take your peecture, I theenk . . .
    God, I need something more than the Gauguin
    clichés of mysterious, heavy-limbed
    unsmiling women.

    And of Vaisala and the Sunday evening films
    of violent Westerns (a surprising end to a day
    of mass prayer and devotional singing) what
    may I say? With my mind's eye taken in
    by the easy grace with which the men and women
    subside cross-legged on the mats, courteously
    making room for others: a discovery
    of the same elements of unfussy calm
    in the way you turned to me with peeled
    segments of mandarin, juice-loaded: my interest
    in the gunfight at the OK Corral phasing
    to a pipless orange dream of petrol generator
    and projector noises: seeing only

the strong-bow palms inclining
to that deep-baying white ministerial
dog collar encircling the harbour's neck:
your profile in the single light bulb
outside: elusive fragrance of frangipani
in the night air

New Zealand Rugby Union

What's in a game?
Apartheid would smell as sweet
If Rugby be thy name.

Martin Luther King

In Vietnam they're using a new rifle shell
that's a real honey. It describes a tumbling
parabola that could punch a hole in you
a foot square, check?

But when that 30.06
made a bloody mash out of your jaw, it didn't
stop there: kept ploughing right on through to
drain the marrow out of your dream.

That bullet wasn't meant to grunt an apology,
the meanie. When you slumped down, mankind
was hurled back a billion years, to a
jellyfish.

Let's face it, King: when news of your death
came through, lovers all over the World
turned each other on, rolled over, and turned
the radio off.

But you were hip. And you never did fancy
fancy-names like Uncle Tom or Handkerchief-head.
You really dug the scene, man. From Birmingham
on you stuck your neck out; opened your big
black beautiful mouth to protest about the high
cost of dying in Vietnam. And you marched

armed only with a dream: a dream held aloft
in your red-hot parable-picking hands. Hell,
your continued existence had become an untidy
question mark sloshed across the American
Declaration of Independence. Yeah: and that
is why they shot you, King.

Before your light was snuffed out, you asked
for a song sung real sweet: hell,
this ain't much. Treacle in my veins: death-cart
rumble in my ears.

Country visit

When I got back from the dunny outside
the place seemed to have come alive. Unattended
a vacuum-cleaner whined but didn't take off.
A pop record jangled and clanged to hip-jerking
finger-snapping nieces: *breakfast, Uncle?*
But when my
dear
little
grandnephew banged
my shin with his tricycle, through clenched
teeth I hissed: not to worry. *Hell, no.*

The sun had climbed higher: I wondered about your
disappearance but sensed that you had gone to the
field of maize and kamokamo which drew me stooping
low through a cut-out in the high hedge.

You had a crooked arm full of puha and I thought:
that is good. And you looked good too moving in the
sun among the flop-eared corn-stalks.
You said angry-like: Lazy kids, these corn should
have been picked long ago. Anyway, we can still
bundle them in sacks and stick some in running water.
Then let us get stuck in, I said, pulling my belly in
like a true warrior.
We started out wrenching a third of the field; piling
the corn into three heaps. I was glad finally when you
decided to move over to where you had dropped the bundle
of puha, and I thought: hell, I'm hungry.

You said, pointing: Do you see that plant, brother?
Can you eat it? I said, looking.
Kapu-a-Rangi: grows like a weed, and good for finding
things out; you had better take a good look.
My eyes clicked like a camera.
It's good listening to you, my sister. Your voice
drugs me: and with the sun scratching my back, I can always
switch off lazy and let the locusts take over jawing their
mouth-bows like crazy

Which didn't matter much because your second
telling helped to underline that what you said
sounded like you thought I was sick, or something.

You said firmly: If the Pakeha doctors cannot
make the pain disappear, you must find this plant,
boil it, and bathe the area of the pain with the
water: if the pain dies down, then you know
someone has been pointing the bone.

I nearly forgot I was hungry.

But soon after, in a house shaking to a pop tune
throbbing, I dangled my grandnephew high and by
the legs because the pain had gone from my shin
and my favourite niece said she would make
doughboys to go with the kamokamo, the meat
and the puha . . .

Bloody good to get home now and again.

Pension day blues

At noon today a sneak-thief dawn wearing dark
    glasses sidled up to me and said: Can I
    buy you a drink?

You've got a familiar face, I lied, pushing my
empty glass foward.
I want you to meet someone, he said, sneaking
a look around the bar. He's not seen you
around for a while.
The more the merrier, I said, raising my glass:
Happy daze . . .

The sneak-thief dawn whistled the sun down
    from his high perch: Meet my brother.
    We touched briefly.
    I am only down for a quick one, the sun
    said. Would you like another?
    It's empty, I said, Filler-up.

When the sun ballooned through the door and up
into the sky again, everyone who had hoped for
an eclipse lowered their dark bottles like
monocles, and turned their backs to us.

Later, with the bar-top awash, the sneak-thief
    dawn began to look like a favourite cousin.
    I had misgivings when he introduced me to
    a couple of hard cases I already knew.
    My sister twilight, he said. And the dark
    sort behind her is our mother:
        o, tell us another one, croaked
        the morepork in the Domain behind
        the hospital.
I'm no good at remembering names,
I said.

The sneak-thief anonymous dawn took off his dark
glasses and ordered a last round for the road.
Well hell, I thought, trying hard to focus, he is
not the rosy-fingered type you read about. A bit
shady looking, even: with dirty finger-nails.

72

His friends were okay: their behaviour impeccable.
    Not a word out of place: I mean, they didn't
    form a tight circle or tell you out of the
    corner of their mouths to piss off . . .

Bus journey, south

Distantly the mountains stand away
radar-like tracking, cutting my ego
down to a pocket-size Gulliver-pebble.
Autumn colours: racehorses: and more
sheep.

The road straightens like an arrow.
My legs shoot out, flop, draw back
again. The bus thunders on but can't
seem to lose the fat-back gold-bearing
animals behind: too much.
Mesmerised my eyes change sides
give up.

The sun tries hard at Ashburton but
lacks feeling. The wind mouths the
stark poplars; whistles the dogs home.
I drag myself after the others to
feed; my mouth slotting a stale Sunday
railway sandwich. *Where have all the
Maori gone, for chrissake?* And I get
a hell of a feeling that if I'm caught
trapping eels under the long bridge
the mountains will rush up to stone me.

The bus takes off belching gears.
Dead leaves lying lightly by the road
rise up, pirouette and collapse in a
twinkling whirlpool of amber light.
I suck my Gulliver-pebble: spit it out
again. Too much.

To a Maori figure cast in bronze outside the Chief Post Office, Auckland

I hate being stuck up here, glaciated, hard all over
and with my guts removed: my old lady is not going
to like it

I've seen more efficient scarecrows in seedbed
nurseries. Hell, I can't even shoo the pigeons off

Me: all hollow inside with longing for the marae on
the cliff at Kohimarama, where you can watch the ships
come in curling their white moustaches

Why didn't they stick me next to Mickey Savage?
'Now then,' he was a good bloke
Maybe it was a Tory City Council that put me here

They never consulted me about naming the square
It's a wonder they never called it: Hori-in-gorge-at-
bottom-of-hill. Because it is like that: a gorge,
with the sun blocked out, the wind whistling around
your balls (your balls mate) And at night, how I
feel for the beatle-girls with their long-haired
boyfriends licking their frozen finger-chippy lips
hopefully. And me again beetling

my tent eyebrows forever, like a brass monkey with
real worries: I mean, how the hell can you welcome
the Overseas Dollar, if you can't open your mouth
to poke your tongue out, eh?

If I could only move from this bloody pedestal I'd
show the long-hairs how to knock out a tune on the
souped-up guitar, my mere quivering, my taiaha held
at the high port. And I'd fix the ripe kotiro too
with their mini-piupiu-ed bums twinkling: yeah!

Somebody give me a drink: I can't stand it

Limerick

An American soldier
From Nantucket
Was issued a broom
And a bucket

In Vietnam
When he saw
The blood and the gore
Checked in his gear
And said: I want

to go home, man: shoot
the police dog
that chawed the hell
out of my kid sister

Haikuku

To reach the dizzy heights
of non-involvement
one must be unattached

In order to reach the peak
of non-attachment (ah yes)
one must be dissolved

Sandra

Today as I step away and out
of myself to look, I wonder
about me and bump: it's your
birthday

Forgive me: but it is not
too late to send a kumara or
book — which seems ordinary

Outside there's a hell of a
struggle going on between my
cabbage tree and the wind.
The sun has already decided
to hit the sack early: the sky
shakes out a white bull-whip
to crack

Well, you may not like
the bullshit and jazz which
sometimes go with the poetry
I write, and if I tell of an
earlier my-time in another place
another country, well hell
I leave you no choice

Another country? Nothing special:
just another way of growing.
Anyway, at fourteen
the contours of the land didn't

interest me much and I only noticed
it when I climbed the hill
to school.
The hill got steeper as the work
became harder.

There were compensations:
I wondered about girls a lot. Grew
kind of secretive when I discovered
I had a flair for growing body hair:

recall the day the sky fell on
my head when the lining of my
pocket broke letting out a sudden
harvest of clay and glass balls
which chattered and bounced
on the school floor:
> *Trevor, Doug, Jimmy, I cried,*
> *and with my voice breaking*
> *into top soprano, screamed:*
> *gimme back me fuckin' marbles*
> *yous kids*

And oh, the hard times
when I used to walk the grey streets
of the city with a face like a
kaka, sardined feet coffined in
shoes too tight for them. Yeah, it's

hard looking back on the wincing
times. But what a good hell it was
to be vulnerable: cry joy alive
to the whip and zip of blood leaping
in the veins.

Girl, I can't write a pretty poem
for your thirteenth birthday.
I write only to thank you for the
plate of raw marinaded fish-flesh
which awakened my taste-buds
yesterday:

and to tell you tonight
of the furl of music unfolding
to the wind's swirl on the cypress
tree next door: imperious rap
of rain on the windows.

Love pome

How beautifully
your fingers interlock: how
decorously decorative.
Must you pick your nose like that?

But how uncommonly comely.

How uncrucially crucial:
shuddering balls! Woman
you unsex me farting glib and
gustily.

O, but how utterly homely.

from

SOMETHING NOTHING

One-way trippers

Graveyards, said the learned man,
are thought to be the beginning
and not the end of all our
journeyings.

This may hold true of tombs which
shelter king and prince together
with their luckless concubines
and slaves. Lavish preparations

arranged by priestly travel agents
for example would include: diverse
weapons, bright flamingos, chariots
with horse. Pots supplied by

thoughtful relatives were filled
with unguents and wine. Despite all
this, the learned man remarked, the
holy planners never really managed

to get the favoured person off
the ground and into space. On the
other hand, one can say with certainty
that lowly folk who occupy less opulent

and unpretentious graves couldn't get
a lousy third-class travel permit.
But one conclusive fact impresses me:
they all . . . are dead.

Walker

A middle-of-the-road man? You could call
me that.

It got a start maybe away back in the Thirties
when I was just a snot-nosed kid walking home

alone from the pictures with my eyes glued
to the black-nothing wall of night and whistling

tuneless organ music to a Frankenstein shuffle
but barefoot scuffing painful stones heaped up

along the middle of the road. And once I remember
a jumpy moon popped out of grim cathedral clouds

to cross itself, making all the tombstones in the
cemetery rear up eerie to the left of me like a

mouth full of bad teeth. And me: blowing like I've
got a very hot potato poised between my lips, and

running out of whistle very fast. Well, they also
call me 'Tightrope' Walker. I don't give a stuff:

I like the view.

Threadbare quote

Fool's gold weigh down
the pockets of my
tattered coat, girl:

my *Tattersall* dreams

A tail for Maui's wife

Hine: I am moved
           as water moved
           by eel's verve
           and impudence

Tuna: *I move with her*
           I move against her
           I move inside her
           She is water

Maui: There, just behind
           the gills, my fingers
           dig his soft belly:
           tighten

           With his body coiling
           hard and shuddery against
           my wrists, I glop eel
           from his hole

           See, wife: I've chewed
           his head off.
           I shall grill him.
           Throw wood on the fire

Hine: You disgust me
           I am nerveless,
           without pulse.
           I am still water.

On a theme by Hone Taiapa

Tell me poet, what happens to my chips
after I have adzed our ancestors
out of wood?

What happens to your waste-words, poet?
Do they limp to heaven, or go down easy
to Raro-henga?

And what about my chips, when they're
down — and out? If I put them to fire
do I die with them?

Is that my soul's spark spiralling; lost
to the cold night air? Agh, let me die
another hundred times: eyeball

to eyeball I share bad breath
with the flared nostrils of the night.
For it's not me I leave behind: not me.

Only the vanities of people;
their pleasure, their wonder and awe
alone remain.

Bite on this hard, poet: and walk careful.
Fragmented, my soul lies here, there: in
the waste-wood, around.

Haiku (2)

To a tree cling
lonely
bird and leaf

Go bird and leaf:
shake
the sad tree

Desdemona

See, our fingers
in the mirror
flexing

like black
and white swans
necking

Ron Mason

Time has pulled up a chair, dashed
a stinging litre from a jug of wine.
My memory is a sluggard.

I reject your death, but can't dismiss it.
For it was never an occasion for woman
sobs and keenings: your stoic-heart

would not permit it. And that calcium-covered
pump had become a sudden roadblock bringing
heavy traffic to a tearing halt.

Your granite-words remain.
Austere fare, but nonetheless adequate for the
honest sustenance they give.

And for myself, a challenge.
A preoccupation now more intensely felt, to tilt
a broken taiaha inexpertly

to my old lady, Hine-nui-te-po, bless the old
bitch: shrewd guardian of that infrequent *duende*
that you and Lorca knew about, playing hard-to-get.

Easy for you now, man. You've joined your literary
ancestors, whilst I have problems still in finding
mine, lost somewhere

in the confusing swirl, now thick now thin,
Victoriana-Missionary fog hiding legalised land-rape
and gentlemen thugs. Never mind, you've taught me
confidence and ease in dredging for my own bedraggled
myths, and you bet: weighing the China experience
yours and mine. They balance.

Your suit has not the right cut for me except around
the gut. I'll keep the jacket though: dry-cleaned
it'll absorb new armpit sweat.

Ad Dorotheum: She and I together found the poem
you'd left for her behind a photograph.

> *Lest you be a dead man's*
> > *slave*
> *Place a branch upon the*
> > *grave*
> *Nor allow your term of*
> > *grief*
> *To extend beyond the fall of its*
> > *last leaf*

'Bloody Ron, making up to me,' she said, quickly.
Too quickly.

But Time impatient, creaks a chair. And from the
jug I pour sour wine to wash away the only land
I own, and that between the toes.

A red libation to your good memory, friend. There's
work yet, for the living.

A death at sea

He died when the sun found a steamy slot
in the sea

He died when the wind's mouth slackened
in sleep

He was dead when the sea came up rough
again, nudging the small boat in; held now

between black fangs of rock, the body bottomed,
feet and lower parts awash in water, and no

sign ever of rowlocks oars or bailer. *Three days
out, sea: hold. Bring him in again.*

Stand away: get back. Let's have a gawp at our
bonnie prince. Remarkable. Eye-sockets picked

clean: mouth and ears pulsing with maggots.
Tomorrow sun and wind will prance and scrape:

and bring back my bonnie to me, to me . . .
the sea intones, drunkenly.

To a kaumatua in hospital, fading

Too few; and rarely now
we come

to visit you, indiscreetly
as the rustle of

exceptional thighs: with
lots of love and lies (yes)

minute and tabloid white
and sinister as spiders.

Thanks for the apple, Lord

Blessed and blooded woman, close-cropped
the minute curl of your short-hair's ends

invite a penetration steadier than a
studied look. Your body in a manner of

speaking is headier than a blend of coarse
ulterior wines. Tell me:

why does your long hair's length waterfalling
twist the piquant mouth of memory?

For curtains drawn at noon no longer flap
a careful damn for that incautious shade and

nuance love's suave adroitness haul down on
all our flambent afternoons: disentangled nights

Beachcomber interviewed

to Barry Crump

You could be right, and it goes for the West Coast
ones too. The black gap-toothed, hard-to-fish beaches
I mean. Dangerous, but they draw me.

No, I don't have a phony thing going for beaches.
You've got to make it with the sea. Only sometimes
people overdo it, by drowning. The old-time Maori had

a respect. Eat the gifts of the sea, raw. That's basic.
Wrap yourself around some of it. Now take this cluster
of mussels for example:

I prise a couple loose, and with one in each palm see,
I clap my hands and crack their hairy heads together.
Then I go *shlup*, and spit the broken bits out after.

What's my think about rubbish on the beaches? Well,
I don't care. All that skitin' and skatin' around on
the zippy petrol boats and beach-buggies don't worry

me as long as they keep the hell clear of small kids
and oldies. And anyway, even in a half-arsed storm,
the sea could heave and vomit up an oil tanker a half

mile long: you with me?
Hell, you still want to know what I think about beaches?
Fuck, what are yah?

Heemi

for James K. Baxter

No point now my friend in telling
you my lady's name.
She wished us well: offered wheels
which spun my son and me like
comets through the lonely night.
You would have called her Aroha.

And when we picked up three young
people who'd hitched their way
from the Ninety Mile Beach to be
with you, I thought: yes
your mana holds, Heemi. Your mana
is love. And suddenly the night
didn't seem lonely anymore.

The car never played up at all.
And after we'd given it a second
gargle at the all-night bowser
it just zoomed on on gulping
easily into the gear changes
up or down.

Because you've been over this road
many times before Heemi, you'd
know about the steady climb ahead
of us still. But once in the tricky
light, Tongariro lumbered briefly
out of the clouds to give us the old
'up you' sign. Which was real friendly.

When we levelled off a bit at the top
of the plateau, the engine heat couldn't
keep the cold from coming in: the fog
swamping thick and slushy, and pressing
whitely against tired eyeballs.

Finally, when we'd eased ourselves
over a couple of humps and down down
the winding metalled road to the river
and Jerusalem, I knew things would be
all right. Glad that others from the
Mainland were arrowing toward the dawn
like us.

Joy for the brother sun chesting over
the brim of the land, and for the three
young blokes flaked out in the back seat
who would make it now, knowing that they
were not called on to witness
some mysterious phenomenon of birth on
a dung-littered floor of a stable

but come simply to call
on a tired old mate in a tent
laid out in a box
with no money in the pocket
no fancy halo, no thump left in the old
ticker.

Field operations

Tenderly, the soldier places
a flower
between the leaves of:
Fixed lines in Modern War.

That book, said the lootenant,
has gotten to be more useful
for wiping the ass, than
crushing the enemy.

I will sit on it, said the soldier.

cummings

if this alone
        were just a static
                    situation
(and we're really
            motoring
                babe)
                        i would consider
        the funny
            hang of you as
                        malnutrition: ah
    but you are woman
                and therefore different hooray × 3
(for *fuck* sake anyway let's taste
            and toast the difference for auld lang syne)

                twin diadems
        of the tragi-comic are your lips
(myself am pulling funny *intensely* faces over your
            blue bitten neck and shoulder) and
        a striking lure is your siren tongue
                between o
                        beautiful shower of

moist clichés
        you are
            are you?
                        and the

man-smell woman-smell musk and salt-tart taste of you
                    aagh
            older than any tang or chinese dynasty
        and although it's not brand new the mock-pathetic
            cry-note is the friendliest of all
                    miaows

and the elegant frenzy of your up and down slow quick
        yair and i really dig that corny horny action
            when you tuck yourself and me
                    away

Kwantung Guest House: Canton

All the way from the border and in the roomy
air-conditioned train, I try sleep. Impossible:
my neck hurts with the swivelling.

The vastness with the colours changing, banded
geometrical and curving off, make lonely the figure
nearby of a peasant with a black and wide-fringed

hat, and another further away with a water buffalo.
With my eyes seduced by the miracle of thousands of
reclaimed *mou* of red earth burgeoning, I wondered,

thinking in terms of a paltry million or two, where
on earth are all the people? Expecting, I suppose,
to see them burst from the ground like

People's Militia units with crimson flags pulsing
in the wind. Now at day's end, I try to sift
impressions. My sifter breaks down: the City laughs.

I'm overwhelmed by the size of my bedroom suite.
Below my window on the second floor, and through a
long thin island of Saliu trees, palm and decorative

shrub, I can see large chunks of coal, glinting in
the rain and banked up along an eight-foot-high
concrete wall. A pathway between doesn't divide,

but unites the scene in an incongruous way. From the
kitchen below voices of varying intensities float up
human and near. I lift the phone and ask for a beer.

Canton: city of workers — and bicycles. Teeming; alive,
and set firmly into a dynamic base built painfully by
their heroic predecessors and revolutionary patriots.

But Canton is a city as drab as any other on a wet
day: with this notable exception. There are no
bill-board advertisements for Coca-Cola, Dutch Shell

And Exxon petroleum products. Instead, a poster high
and as wide as a building, flaunting a brigade of
coal miners surging. But night has slipped a marker

in closing the Day Book. Tiny lights burning
intermittently among the leaves of the Saliu trees
fade and reappear. *What are they?*

I fight sleep remembering only the urgent bus and
truck horns blurting, underlining proletarian forms
and priorities. I think of Yellow Flower Hill

and the shattered bones of seventy-two revolutionary
martyrs buried there. At least they sleep easier now.
For I am startled by these wide-awake thought-shifts

occasioned by the newness and press of contrasts.
Like the Saliu trees and black coal gleaming: visually
unlike, and with thousands of years between them:

but indivisible, like fire and hammerblow.

A fall of rain at Mitimiti: Hokianga

Drifting on the wind, and through
the broken window of the long house
where you lie, incantatory chant
of surf breaking, and the Mass
and the mountain talking.

At your feet two candles puff the
stained faces of the whanau, the vigil
of the bright madonna. See, sand-whipped
the toy church does not flinch.

E moe, e te whaea: wahine rangimarie

Mountain, why do you loom over us like
that, hands on massive hips? Simply
by hooking your finger to the sea,
rain-squalls swoop like a hawk, suddenly.
Illumined speeches darken, fade to metallic
drum-taps on the roof.

Anei nga roimata o Rangipapa.

Flat, incomprehensible faces: lips moving
only to oratorical rhythms of the rain:

quiet please, I can't hear the words.
And the rain steadying: black sky leaning
against the long house. Sand, wind-sifted
eddying lazily across the beach.

And to a dark song lulling: *e te whaea, sleep.*

Soochow 1973

Worker-artisans have restored the ancient buildings
formerly mis-used by the Kuomintang Cavalry.
Before us the Parks stretch out lovely in the afternoon.

People with their children move easily around
studying the goldfish, sucking ices, or talking over
cups of green tea.

There's space, despite the artfully concertina-ed
perspectives. Compact vistas, hand-formed, beautiful:
a minor insurrection.

And everywhere and for us, the tiny applause from
children with faces lit up like sunflowers. Adopted
and transported, our new names are: Uncle and Auntie.

Chairman Mao writes: 'Revolution is not a dinner party'
And from this I gather, neither is embroidery, nor the
painful density of poetry making, spade-tossed, winnowed.

On Little Hill, I listen vainly for '. . . the cicadas, the
bamboo growing quieter'. Reflect, that although I am not
a true communist (I do not have that steel-sure,

purple-toughened beauty) it is enough that communists
accept my ugliness and truth; defer occasionally to an
accidental line of verse when a poem kicks.

But for dinner tonight I will savour a slice or two
of the lotus root, crisp and white. A small child again
dribbling a haunted taste. Sweet, and a little like

crushed lily stalks.

White Opossum

Ah: let the memory of sweet bird-flesh
tighten nerve and eye.
Let the squeals of fat pig dying caress
the ear.
Sacred opossum: don't punish us today.
Should you appear the hunt must stop
and there will be no meat for the village
fires. Take pity on us, white opossum.

Down by the sea's edge, and in the man-made
harbour, big steel ships wait.

A tortuous bed of white stones is the mountain
road to the sea.
And up from the sea they come by way of the wide
white road.
Inconsolable men, red-skin and white: up they
come to raze the villages, level the forests,
gouge deep wounds, pipe grey earth over the saddle.
Strangers, on the strange machines.

And of prized feathers; cowrie shells from the
sea,
are these of less importance then, than this
anomalous and sad confusion of men who seek
a special kind of dirt, white opossum?

Above us an iron machine hovers, flitting here
there and everywhere like an ugly dragonfly.
Can you hear it, white opossum?
A disturbing clacking obscenity of sound.

Load by piecemeal load, the steel machines huff
and carry your white house away.
Day and night they're blasting the immense white
dome of your house.

The huge boulder that was your citadel
is a graveyard road of white stones to the sea.
They've turned you out of your house, white
opossum.

Down to the sea's edge, and to the man-made
harbour, black steel ships loll easy.

In the early seventies I worked at Panguna, a copper-mine on the island of
Bougainville, as a boilermaker-welder, monitored by the Australian Trade Union
Council. I was glad to get out after six months!

Final memo

1)   tell my competitors
they're shot of me at last:
they can all go back to their
own basic gold-lined insecurities
and hell

2)   remind those socialistic
trade union shits that so long as
my loyal and willing staff keep
their heads lowered
their arseholes pointing steadily
to the skylight, they will never
take-over MY toothbrush factory

3)   pack a toothbrush

4)   I leave now without prejudice
without hatred without fear
without halitosis:

       to my first and only love I return
to the womb of the goose that laid
the golden egg: amen

Ian Fraser

Ian said yesterday
my eyes looked like oysters
close together; smoked.

I can't see too good today.
I've just swallowed
my oysters.

A korero on the beach with Phyllis

On the mud flats near Huia with an ebb tide
thinning the cockle-beds, we watch the pied
oystercatchers long-beaking

the crabs in their holes. Neat. There are
no ecstatic screams. Supremely indifferent
they swing long thin beaks from side to side

like mine-detectors.
They do not hop about like sparrow or blackbird.
Step by sure step they walk with the precise

elegance and assurance of the military. I bend
my back. Ankle-deep in water how reassuring
to hear the knock and rattle of cockle in the

flax kit as I strain black sand away.
Have they got a bend to their beaks? you ask.
But I have never catched a pied oystercatcher

and after another look, I reply: No, their beaks
are straight. Nonetheless, I keep an uncertainty
about this to myself changing the subject.

Somewhere around, I explain, there's another
variety of shellfish four times bigger than a
cockle, dark blue in colour with a fragile shell:

living six inches below ground, they're *really*
into the clay. I am not optimistic. I dredge up
more cockles to make sure of a feed.

However, I intone, their position may be located
by big holes spaced further apart and cleared
regularly by satellite crabs to enable the fish

to feed on plankton when the tide is in.
Faintly triumphant you bellow: I've found one.
I join the hunt. I'm pissed-off. Interesting things

are happening to other-bodies: recall a time
before when you cried out after salvaging a dead
blue-gum leaf floating by with a half-drowned

cicada clinging to it miles and bloody miles
away from Australia.
A conspiracy of time and turn of tide?

A coincidence of furrowed brows in deep obeisance
to some ancient call of sea, benign sky?
Ah, a dream-feast in my mind already, of fish stew

spiked, well-spiced, steaming . . .
Two-dozen-oystercatchers pie-d in a crust, please?

Hay fever

It wasn't the wind
that shook the barley

but Jennifer threshing
and Charlie piling

from

MAKING A FIST OF IT

Children's tale

The taniwha breathes fire
and hot stones.
The taniwha snorts hot dust
and steam.
Golden snot trickles from
his nostrils.

Deep inside the Earth
the taniwha takes deep-breathing
exercises to keep in good shape
for when he has to remind us all
that we are not as powerful as he.

His name is: RU-AU-MOKO.
He is the boss of all the taniwha.

He doesn't give a fart for anyone
or anything. But when he does —
WATCH OUT!

The Earth won't be able to contain
itself.
Earth Mother will split her sides
with laughing.

Reign rain

Neither juggernaut
man
nor crawling thing
with saintliness and ease

can bring
a mountain weeping
to its knees
quicker than rain:

that demure leveller
ocean-blessed
cloud-sent
maker of plains.

Sun o (1)

Coming out sudden as he did
from an amber glut
of morning clouds, lavish

spread his gold around the yard
where hens foregathered
leggily expectant; disappointed

to find the grains light-hearted,
infuriatingly impeccable:
the cock crowing raspy raspberries

jaunty strut
as any rubber-legged captain
on the slips.

Maui makes it
with the Death Goddess

1

My cock install
My life in thrall
In thee I thrust
Indeed I must.

2

'Who saw him die?'
'I,' said the fantail,
flip-flop. 'I saw
him die,' plip-plop.
'Laughed my bloody head off
when he got the chop.'

A know-all nose

As any local grower knows
Autumn roses
In a Parnell garden blows

And he who rashly presupposes
Autumn roses to belong
Exclusively to noses

May reluctantly conclude
That roses
Are indifferent to noses

                *

When a tricky
Politician decomposes
I know why
Fat blowfly blowses.

O, I should ask God
If he knows
Why cold noses
In the winter blowses.

O, go to blowses
Autumn roses.

117

Song to a herdsman's son

Take me Westward, horse. Follow
the sun. Race to the top of
the hill. Face the sun.

My fast horse: my strong horse,
you're invincible. Don't let the sun
set. Hurdle

the oceans, horse. Encircle the
earth. Let me embrace the World's
People: follow the sun.

But get me back in time
to make my father, my mother,
fragrant breakfast-cups of salted
tea with millet — a glass of
hot milk for my baby sister.

This poem was written after a visit to Inner Mongolia, People's Republic
of China, in September/October 1973.

Black Rock, Melbourne

Last night
    you showed me drawings
    of horses marble-necked
    and still: fugitives from
    a Fun Fair merry-go-round.

They look immaculate; complacent,
    groomed by a thousand child-fingers
    smeared with ice-cream
    and candy.

'I can't draw their legs properly, yet,'
    you said.

Justine,
    the eternal Seasons weaken
    fall down tributary
    to your toothy grin.

Ani Rose

I won't cry . . . You just blew it, girl.
Blue/d/it, ya hear? Hell, you just upped

and left your loving kids behind; your lipstick,
atomizer, asthma pills and hair shampoo.

In dying inches you left miles and bloody
miles of loving man friends sprawling, with

oldies like myself huffing after; your lips
sweet tasting as the tawhara — and as succulent;

your words, prodding sentinels waking us, were
also words itching us to a kapai koru line of

laughter. Ah, easy listening, Ani. Easy listening.
And will you remember those craggy wind-swept

dreams you shared with us? Ay?
Bold dreams to build wondrous cities of the mind

rich and searching, and always with the heart
looping-the-loop over, around, and through all

our doings (O Jesus, how unfaithful you are, Ani).
The hell with it, I won't cry —

How *dare* you die, Ani
How dare you die . . .

Poet on a night train

Ah, carefully
let me rephrase my rail-signs: ONE-WAY.
Create new Branch Lines (yes)
Place coal-fired locomotives steaming on
every Line (beaut)
Reroute them all (right) that way
I cannot lose myself.

Yea: and just about now I'm tracking down
the ancient detour lines of laughter; up-
tilt lines for the crying to wash away
imaginary grit in the eyes.

DING — DINg — Ding — Ding — ding — din — di — d . . .

Stationmaster, raise the barriers. Tell me
when may I stick my hand up for the
U-Turn?
Soon (klackety-klack)?
Later? (hey, where the hell are we?)
Or at some impossible journey's end where
clammily there will always be a washed-up
improbable dawn to greet me.

And looking out again through reflective
glass, see looming
as moving tree-groups in the mist, the squat
gainliness of a barn, a house, holding hands
together and sleepwalking.

But it was only me after all (and the World
going in the opposite direction) ka-klackety
klacking along still on
the rails.
Ah . . .

Slaughter on Kiwi Avenue

When I returned from what I might characterise
as a last nervous piss, she said, turning the
ignition on, 'Do you mind?'

'You're in the box seat,' I said.
'The boot is on the other foot, now,' she said,
leaning determinedly on the accelerator.

'Then let it be on your head,' I said, as we
slithered heatedly across the street slap-bang
into the expensive plate-glass purple

sign-painted *EXCELSIOR PET EMPORIUM* as it came
down magical like brittle guillotine blades, and
WHOA-oh-oh-oh, I think I said, and resigned . . .

She wore a plain golden ring on her finger, and
a pigeon cooing in her hair where the boot should
have been, or alternatively planted

accurately but firmly up her jaxie.
'My chickens, my chickens,' yelled the lady in
the Emporium like they were already coloured

blue, and murdered. 'Hell, don't count on them,'
I said, weakly. A coy flop-eared mutt ambled over
to lick the blood off my face.

'Can you switch the motor off?' someone said,
pulling the dog away before it could chew off my
nose. 'Your mate is out

like a light,' he said.
Oh, bloody original, I thought. She's missed the
bus again.

O Africa

On bloody acts
that make less human
mankind's brighter sun,
let revulsion rise.
Eclipse the moon's
black evil: so that

innocence and the child
shall reign
so that we may dream
good dreams again.

Making a fist of it

Soweto, Alexandra, Alice: Johannesburg, June/July 1976

A black girl-baby soft and beautiful involuntarily
    stiffens waking herself from sleep. Wide-eyed
    she greets strange objects around her with a shy
    diffidence; gurgles hello and is suddenly convulsed.
    Everything seems terribly funny.

Remembering fingers press vainly into slack breasts
    of air for food. A hungry baby-mouth orbiting will not
    rendezvous today nor lock on to a nose-cone nipple.
    Gurgling sounds trail off . . .

Untidily, and in abandonment her mother lies in the dusty
    unsealed street, a police bullet buried hungrily
    between her breasts.

The black girl-baby soft and beautiful reaches for her
    rattle; discovers it in the strange harsh sounds coming
    from her father's lungs enriched with gold-dust and
    tear gas.

Daddy, give it to me. Let me have a play?

Making fists of rage the black girl-baby no longer soft or
    beautiful kicks; her kicking has become hard and ugly.
    Sex trembling, her fingers open as if prised apart. Like
    a flower a gun blossoms in her hands. A silence gathers
    just like people going to a sullen meeting — or funeral.
    Whose, I wonder?

The diamond-mine owners shrug sleek immaculate shoulders
    and though the day be hot suppress a shiver:
    What the hell are those black policemen doing?
    GODVERDOMME!

They will have to move quickly — more quickly, you know.
    Yes, and more firmly . . .

GODVERDOMME! Three thousand blacks absent from work today! Seventy transport buses burnt and destroyed! Profits will plummet. Rome, Paris — yes, and the Bahamas vacation holiday is OUT this year.

The silence deepens. A silence as ominous as that which follows sky-sizzle thump and crackle of thunder in the distance. Or, a sound somewhere inside the cavern of the ear, quite close — like the cocking of a gun . . .

Rifle-butt firm on the ground for support, the black girl-baby is climbing up. She has only one knee on the ground now. Behind her black work-hardened hands fist a forest of rifles, waving . . .

See, the black girl-baby is standing up: beautiful.

Papa-tu-a-nuku (Earth Mother)

We are stroking, caressing the spine
    of the land.

We are massaging the ricked
    back of the land

with our sore but ever-loving feet:
    hell, she loves it!

Squirming, the land wriggles
    in delight.

    We love her.

This poem refers to the Awakening — the Maori land march that began at
Te Hapua, the northernmost settlement of Te Aupouri, on 14 September 1975
and ended at Parliament Buildings, Wellington, on 17 October.

Rain-maker's song for Whina

I'll not forget your joints creaking as you climbed into
the bus at Victoria Park to bless the journey.
When you broke down in the middle of the Lord's Prayer,
I thought that what you left unsaid hung more tangibly
uncertain above us all than some intangible certainty
that we would all get a comfortable berth in the
hereafter.

Saint Christopher in the rain at night, just before Mangamuka
Gorge. People wearing Saint Christopher badges getting
off the bus and helping to put an overturned vehicle right
side up. No one hurt. I finger the cheap badge you gave me
of the saint. *Will it be all right?*

A couple of days later in bright sunshine, we hit the road
leaving Te Hapua behind. And all the way south — to the
'head of the fish', I picked up some hard truths embedded in
your hilarious speeches on the marae:

> *No more lollies! We been sucking the Pakeha lolly*
> *for one hundred and fifty years.*
> *Look at what's happened. Look at what we got left.*
> *Only two millon acres. Yes, that's right. Two million*
> *acres out of sixty-six million acres.*
> *Think of that. Good gracious, if we let them take what*
> *is left we will all become taurekareka. Do we want that?*
>
> *So you listen, now. This is a sacred march. We are*
> *marching because we want to hold on to what is left.*
> *You must understand this. And you must think of your*
> *tupuna. They are marching beside you. Move over, and*
> *make room. We are not going to Wellington for nothing.*
> *And don't be mistaken: Kare tenei hikoi oku, he hikoi*
> *noa-aha ranei-ki te miri-miri i nga paoro o Te Roringi.*

E, kui! What a way to bring the 'House' down. You could not
have lobbed a sweeter grenade. I'm all eared-in to you,
baby . . . *Kia ora tonu koe.*

Maniapoto

Through the cut hill, high above the awakened town,
the road turns before tipping over.
The heat-shimmer shifty on the sealed road makes black
delusive pools.

Hung out bare and fidgety on the aching branches of a
poplar tree, two small boys raise a ragged cry.
I adjust the camera-eye for a long shot.

Wavery above the heat-shimmer I see the top of the
pou-whenua emerging. To a swarthy afternoon breeze —
a white flag pulsing silkily.

Blistered feet are slapping the sealed road. Sore feet
hongi an endless greeting to loose stones scattered by
the road-side.

Over the cut hill the marchers swing into the camera
frame; heads bobbing; thigh muscles protesting a new
braking action.

*Te Kuiti: (Te Kuiti-tanga a nga whakaro . . .) my thoughts
gallop to a focal point there.*
'Learn to do the humble tasks first,' the old people say.
*I scrub the lavatory bowls, visit the cemetery, pick up match-
sticks and cigarette-ends before leaving the marae.*

Thinly and far off a question mark hangs forlornly in the air
as the ngarara train rolls out of the station.
Te Awamutu, Kihikihi, Otorohanga, Te Kuiti,

we leave you our koha-gifts of forgotten singlets and
        underpants
drying on the barbed-wire fence, together with our love and
broken sandals:

your tuna and puha kisses, we take with us.

Street march and demonstration, Dunedin, 14 October 1977

How classically subversive! Red penis-heads of tulips
opening at last to vibrant vulvas, publicly, and on a mildly
raucous evening at the Octagon.

We ask the City Authorities to rope off the tulip-beds
afraid in case agents provocateurs should infiltrate the collective
anger of rough talk and protest speeches treacle off as weak as
trout's piss.

Robert Burns' statue puts on a cold front.
He has something more pungent to say about the faceless overstayers
traitorous, richer and more powerful than Parliament. The leading
marionette, Corporal Muldoon, will walk on water all the way
to Taiwan — before drowning.

We clap our hands, turn and clap each other — and the piper
who led us here. Next week he will be spied on. There's a man going
around taking names. Of course the inevitable will happen. Prison
walls will come apart in an immense cloud of falling masonry, and to
a bagpipe under a tartaned armpit, clenching.
SCOTS WHA HAE . . .

Ah, how good to sense the first awakening flicker of
muscularity in the trees' arms. Indeed, how magical they seem in the
street lights with spring fuzz bursting all over and thinning
to delicate twigs — scratch marks in a bland sky.

We pick up the debris of the protest march, stuff left over
placards into litter bins, together with hot phrases thought about
but never aired. We have to brave the cold, sometime; open more
windows to let the stink of fear sidle out.

Erotically, tulips yawn; limp heads closing and knowing
neither classicism nor subversion.

After 151 days of rain, things became a lot clearer . . . (weather report)

to Dick Scott

You've climbed down off your high perch, rain.
I'm sorry. My attention riveted elsewhere,
I missed your stately march down the valley;
a man on stilts, striped pants billowing.
But how do you cure a headache, rain? See!
Armed marines, steel-helmeted — running.

That day in the streets, batons whistled just
like a tui strangling; a wharfie crumpled
in the gutter with blood rushing to his face.

You've washed your hands clean. So, why lean
fulsome now on broken window-glass? How
bloody futile. You can't know everything, rain.

Dick Scott is the author of *151 Days*, a significant and sympathetic account of the waterside workers' lockout by employers in 1951.

from

YEAR OF THE DOG

Lines to a better poet

Curious indeed to find not even a photo of you
in my house to fix for a while
in the memory.

In your own tight measure — sprung elegance,
you'd rephrased all the verities.
Released at last you were free:

The income tax department owed you
money. There was nothing in the way of tinned
accoutrements — the jink and clunk of high

office. All that would have been meaningless
junk to you and quite superfluous. My memory
of you momently derailed, I remember only

someone ineffectual salvaging a wet speech;
rain flurries sweeping in from the north,
and smoothing out to a blue threat without heart

or heat to it.
Your destination unlabelled,
I reach down for a fistful of ritual earth. Not

so strange after all to leap at the only chance
to throw mud at you gravely
at your grave's edge.

A song in praise
of a favourite humming-top

I polish your skin. It is that of a woman
    mellowed by the oil of the tarata,
    humming-top. What stable secret do you

    keep locked up in movement, humming-top?
    skipping away daintily as you do, sidewise
    lurching, nonchalantly coming erect?

Your drowsy sighs lull and beguile the people
    the many, who've come to hear your talk,
    your whizz your buzz your angry bee-stung

    murmurs — which are simply about nothing
    at all. Ah, see: they're closing in —
    stopping just short of whip range.

Eyeballs plopping like bird's eggs sucked
    deep into your whirlpool, they're surging
    forward again treading on each other's feet.

Lips stretched tightly over teeth, they grin;
    find throat at last to shout; exclaim.
    O, they will leave finally, when they've

    finished fondling you, cooing over you like
    a kukupa. I don't like it: each one of them
    a thief's heart gladdened — but covetous.

This poem developed from a 'Spell for a wooden humming-top cut out
and fashioned from a totara; matai. Woods which alone hum and whine
beautifully'. Author unknown. Text in Edward Shortland's Maori Manuscript
Notebook 2(b) (MS2), 73, Hocken Library, University of Otago, Dunedin.

Refuge in Akarana Avenue

for Vonnie

East wind from afar conducts
    a small *canzona*;
    an orchestration of karaka,
    guava, plum and peach leaves
    prancing; the special oval
    sounds that are lemons;
    the globular poor man's orange.

How may I forget them?
    The gentle concave
    of a filled creek-bed smoothed
    by a hand-mower; the burp and
    snuckle of frog and eel —
    distanced from me now — echoing
    still?

Variegated tree-leaf shapes spinning,
    dapple my skin, wincing to shadows
    kindlier than needling light-pecks
    from the sun; blue freckles
    falling from a filtered moon.
    Ah, but how easy

    to recall the backyard orchard,
    the incinerator made of concrete
    building blocks, the red
    garden table burgeoning with food
    where good talk flowers bonding
    the ease of decision; the complex
    of a simple plan. A matter
    of practice; matter of fact.

Cross-eyed

to Ron Mason

And outside the gates milling, were the halt,
    the lame, and the loud-mouthed admirers
    who tomorrow would pounce with great noise
    and throw their crutches at Him.

    This notwithstanding, and secure in the
    curious knowledge that all would come right
    in the end, committed, chose the path of
    thorns and shriek of torn flesh nailed to
    the crossed wood.

Only in the mindless far-stretched agony, agony
    of flesh, did His eyeballs to the yellow
    heavens roll to complain mildly of desertion.

    Though He would be the last to recognise it,
    the heavens smirking will recoil
    in embarrassment at His sad moment of truth.

O, what useless appendages the realities are to
    the starry-eyed.

Insomniac

One eye Cyclopean squinting up against the sun, I watch
a skylark build a spiral staircase of love-song.
It's seasonal I suppose; trite. Embarrassed, the sun
retreats, skidding down

the far side of blue hill losing some skin: for
neither singer nor song is for him — or moonlight
cocktail-gushers, either. *O, how long must this
torture go on?* Of course,

the after-life of song goes on — the spiral
staircase is dismantled, cascading notes imprinted
indelibly on the evening air. And now . . . crickets;
dental drills whining in my brain:

tikiti-tikiti totoko, piripi-piripi

I eavesdrop on fat morepork calling each other up:
'We're heading for the mice round-up' they chorus.
How droll. They've got pig's trotters on the brain,
too. An abandoned abattoir of pork-longing. An owl's
house of baleful whos. Beleaguered,

I sleep with one eye open,
waiting
for Odysseus to come. A burning brand — oblivion:
anything. Quite maddening.

Steam loco on siding

Huffily, the southbound engine detaches itself, gleaming.
The southbound engine sidles off to the water tower
for a long drink. It is a black swimmer doing
the sidestroke, huge steel arms pistoning.

REFRESHMENTS. For most, a journey not yet concluded.
Time out for the wet-lipping of thick railway mugs
of yellow tea. In it, the sugar spoon stands upright
and perfectly still. I point to an adhesive jam roll;
a hardboard meat pie. The lady behind the counter
looks at me sadly and grunts. Indifferently, I grunt
back — and pay up. A whistle shrills. The scrum
breaks up in the Refreshment Rooms.

ALL ABOARD, BED 'n BAWD . . . I can feel the long steel
vertebrate shake and shudder. The southbound engine is
coupling once more with the Leading First Class
carriage. Tensing, I settle suddenly and deeply
in my seat, a jam roll jammed up my nostrils.

Complacent steel arms folded, the southbound engine
snoozes, waking briefly to exchange steamy insults
with the diesel-fired northbound train coming in.

Fanfare: the stationmaster appears. Tumultuous
silence. He looks directly at me and holds up the back
of his right hand. One rigid middle finger is pointing
straight up. Puzzled. I say to myself: so? ONE what?
It is a signal. The station moves forward. We track it.
The stationmaster beckons. The station returns and goes
to the rear. Frantically backing, we track it.

The stationmaster takes one neat step back. Drum roll.
He looks to his left and then to his right. Superb.
He is conducting an orchestra. He adjusts his cap, his
tie, and blows his whistle. All glowy and grimy, the
station reappears: *kiss my arse says the northbound
train, leaving.* Stunned, I look at the writing on the
end wall.

New Zealand Government Railway
warns, indeed expects, that no
man pee, nor expectorate while
            the train is not in motion.

Desolate, we are left standing.

A talk with my cousin, alone

And afterwards, after the shedding of mucus, the droll
    speeches and the hongi for my cousin in the box,
    we were called to meal at the long tables.
    But I hadn't come for that.

I could hear the Tasman combers shredding themselves
    nearby, wishing then for a cawing beak of sound
    to help me reassemble myself. Taking my shoes off,
    I trudge a steep dune; sand, a cool silken lisp
    spilling through my toes.

Bottomed on a hill of sand, I wondered wry dry leaves
    whether the Pakeha marine authorities would sell
    us back ephemeral Maori land (now exposed to bird,
    bleached crab and shrimp) lying somewhere between
    low-water mark and high.

A pounding gavel is the sun today — a brassy auctioneer:
    the sea, his first assistant. Of this, no instant
    favour offered me in stint. I cushion my elbows
    deeper in sand. I'm the only bidder.
    For this beautiful piece of land/seascape, I will
    start the bidding at twenty falling axes per square
    centimetre, said the sun looking hard at me for an
    earlobe twitch, or, other sign.
    Get stuffed, I reply, holding my middle finger
    straight up — turning it. Slowly.

Idly I think, that after the eleven o'clock prayers
    tomorrow (and before lunch) my cousin will have
    gone to ground.
    'They may ban tangi-hanga in the future,' I say
    to him. 'Right now you're doing your job. This
    moment is forever as the splayed fingers of the hand
    drawn together, like a fist.' I look up at the sun
    and blink. The sun is beside itself, dancing. There
    are two of them.

Old comrade

to Jim Jamieson

Like frightened girls, the years
ran in thickening to panic-stations
and the days ran out for Jim
as he walked past them, and beyond.

Why, only a few days ago, hatless,
immaculately tied and overcoated,
head-on, Jim shouldered his way out
of the Crown and into the wind
at the corner of Rattray Street: he
didn't hear me call out. Jim was
ghosting.

Shoulders hunched, tartan scarf whipping,
Jim leaned into the wind. The wind leaned
right back and then pulled away. Jim fell.
He didn't feel the hardness or coldness
of the pavement, for, like an old friend
come back, the wind held him as he fell.

Well, there was no magic tolling of the
bell, and the skies never opened up. But
the ground did . . .
At the graveside, no one wanted to add
or subtract. No one — except the capitalist,
who never even looked up from counting
his worthless paper-money. But, you know . . .

I reckon old Marx would make room for him;
Lenin, throw another log on the fire;
and Mao, like a full moon rising pour a bowl
of tea, offer Jim a cigarette. Bet on it.

He waiata whakahōnore atu ki a Haki rāua ko Hōhepa

I waenganui o te Pō maringi mai ngā roimata
    o te Rangi. Ka tino whakakopeke au ki a' au anō.
    Te nui hoki o taku hiahia ki te moe tonu.
I taku whakahāwea atu — tino kino rawa te riri
    a te āwhā. Kangakangātia ahau.
    Whakaomaomangia ngā pū nunui o te
    Rangi. Pakopakō mai te haere. Tahuna
    kia kā te Ao. Whātero mai — pūkana mai ana.

Nā te hau tonga kē ahau i whakaoho. Patua ōku
    taringa — turi tonu. Ko taku whakamīharo rawa
    i te kaha o te hau ki te hamahama i te rino o te
    whare. Te taimaha hoki o te pātōtō mai i te kūaha.

E tama, kei hea ō hoa ināianei?
    Ō hoa ngotengote kina, ngotengote wheua, pihikete,
    mātenga ika. Ō hoa kua ngaro noa atu ngā niho.
Kei hea rāua ināianei? Ō hoa kaha ki te kai rama?
    Ō hoa kōwhetewhete — rawe ki te whakamārama
    moemoeā — peti hōiho?
Kei hea ō koroheke? O Pāpā ki te pupuri i ētahi
    taonga mōu? Ētahi anō ō tātou i whiwhi i te
    tūranga kaitiaki i te Mauri o te iwi?
E tama, mehemea kua haere ō koroheke ki te
    koraha ngaro noa iho — kia tere!
    Tikina! Rapua!

Ka hou anō te whakaaro ki ahau, i rā pea, he tikanga
    anō kei roto i ngā tohu kua pā mai ki ahau.
Puta atu ahau ki waho, ki mua o te whare
    mihi haere ana, karakia ana, waiata ana.
E mihi ana ki a wai?
    Ki ngā papi-kurī o te Rangi e mitimiti ana
    nei i ōku roimata?

Ki te hau tonga kua whakahurihia ki tua?
    Rapua. Rapua te tikanga a ngā kupu o te Pō.
    Haruru tonu te pararē mai a te moana:
    Āe hoki, āe. Māku tēnā e āmine, e tautoko atu.

Kāhore i mau i a' au te pātai a te whenua, ngā kupu
      teitei ā ēnei maunga a Whakarongorua rāua
      ko Tokatoka. Kāhore i whakarongo atu i te auē
      mai a te ngahere, te tangi hotuhotu a ngā
      kukupā o Taiamai, te ngongorō whakaoho kino
      o ngā kūaka kua whakarērea nei te
      pito o te oneone.

Haere e koro mā, haere.
      Kīhai i mōhio tā kōurua tamaiti kua heke noa atu
      kōurua ki te kōpū o te whenua.
      Haere e Hōhepa. O karakia tawhito, i hipokina
      mai ki runga i tōku mātenga — e tiaki tonu
      ana i ahau.
      E Haki, nōku tonu tō ingoa, i hōmai
      e koe kia ora ahau.
      Pai noa iho. Whakarerea tā kōurua
      tamaiti hei toenga mō te Ao.
      Pō, pō, ao tonu.

I wish to thank John Waititi for his help in checking this poem.

143

Tiaki: independence fighter

to J. & J. E.

Of course, always, and
following each raw and savage
battle,
it was you who twitched
the down-turned corners of the
lips to wan smiles,
set tired feet to rhythmic flexing;
the land sky-bumping

And now, utterly faceless, yourself
laid low, lowly, we lower you lower
than the breathy breathless note of
the mute bone flute placed in your
lifeless fingers

Conditions permitting (of course) and
unmenaced by a friendly silence,
we chant your songs with steely gusto,
sometimes stirring from
a drunken thicket and mist a
dark owl in sad voice, asking
asking

the contours of your face
uneasily, we've forgotten.

Annie

I am filled with your
richness and my remorse
(just now thickening
to a boil on my right ear)

I get down on my elbows
and knees, left . . . right,
left . . . right, painfully
picking up yesterday's apples
with my teeth; impossible.

But for my snot-shuffles
there is only a vast silence.
A space palpable and empty.

You've gone.
I read your note once more.
It is crumpled and smoothed
out again. You've gone. The
space you've left is
unbearable: I keep tripping
over it. Forgive me

but I do not want to lead
nor have you walk in front
and in my long shadow.

Come back. Walk on my
left side, heart-side; close:
the sun a noon-crown without
shadow

Lovers

On the occasion of a visit to New Zealand
by Germaine Greer

In a packed house we pressed
into a knee-high row
of seats. It was hot.

The chairman began again
when we were quite settled.
I sniffed. Fastidiously.

Indifferent, you blamed me
for using all the hot water.
Then, you should have
showered with me, I muttered.

It's a you-and-me smell, you
said with deliberation,
breast heavy-loll against me.

Arms lowly, and beseeching
heaven, I juggled my eyeballs;
your lizard-eyes fixed wise
on me.

The speaker was a woman who spoke
plainly, but only one plain
word I caught from her all
evening. I think she said fuck:

and O,
said everyone turning to look
at us.

Status-seeker

After Chuan Tzu, 3rd century, B.C.

And who should come scrabbling up
the other side of the hill but old beam face, Ra
himself sweating to keep his appointment — for
chrissake — but using the springiness of trees to
catapult himself off the top of the hill sailing over
over us oho like a giant frog in yellow tights criss-
crossing his legs in the air like ballet star Nijinsky
and shooting sparks out of his tail blinding his pale
companion, Marama, pacing him like an actor without
a speaking part and carrying a sparkling scythe
recently polished.

The stars have moved nearer
circling coyly like an obedient procession
of funerary jewels suitably distanced from each other
and numbered so that each may be joined to look like a
crab a dog a bear a goat a broken calabash, a spoon
a runaway dish and dairy cow Sloppy running loose
and dropping hot pancakes for the ghost riders in the
sky with everyone chanting hosannas like olés pulsing
up from the marae-arena and everybody I mean every
body going absolutely bananas leaping up and throwing
their potaes and lavalavas high in the air pushing
and shoving to get the last word in before the big
eclipse at exactly 2.37 p.m. when a very confused
rooster will crow his head off again three times
for deaf Peter and I tell you if all heaven and earth

is a holy parenthesis

then I shouldn't mind one bit if my tapu my mana
my ihi my soul were encompassed by it. Nor would
I want to add another thing except to listen to a
crazy poet singing off-key off-beat hymns of
dubious character as I choke in vast merriment;
my sober translation — a misting away into
that which is both mythical and magical
and beyond folklore.

The river is an island

You are river. This way and that
and all the way to sea two escorts
shove and pull you. Two escorts
in contention.

Left bank or right bank, how can
you be a river without either?

Thus are U-bends made. Thus are
S-bends made. Your direction
is assured and sometimes running
perfectly and quite straight.

A low bank on your left holds your
laughing stitches in. On your right
side skips another hushing your
loud protests.

You are river. Joy leaping down
a greenstone stairway: anger cradled
in a bed of stones.

You're a harbour; a lake; an island
only when your banks lock lathered
arms in battle to confine you: slow-release you.

Go river, go. To ocean seek your
certain end. Rise again to cloud;
to a mountain — to a mountain
drinking from a tiny cup.
Ah, river

you are ocean: you are island.

Snowfall

It didn't make a grand entrance and I nearly
missed it — tip-toeing up on me as it did
when I was half asleep and suddenly, they're there
before my eyes — white pointillist flakes
on a Hotere canvas — swirling about on untethered

gusts of air and spreading thin uneven
thicknesses of white snow-cover on drooping
ti-kouka leaves, rata, a lonely kauri, pear
and beech tree. Came without hesitation
right inside my opened window licking my neck

my arms my nose as I leaned far out to embrace
a phantom sky above the house-tops
and over the sea: *'Hey, where's the horizon?*
I shall require a boat you know — two strong arms?'
. . . and snow, kissing and lipping my face

gently, mushily, like a pet whale,
or (if you prefer) a shark with red bite — sleet
sting hot as ice. Well,
it's stopped now. Stunning sight. Unnerved,
the birds have stopped singing,

tucking their beaks under warm armpits: temporarily.
And for miles upon whitened miles around,
there is no immediate or discernible movement,
except from me, transfixed, and moved by an interior
agitation — an armless man applauding.

'Bravo,' I whisper. 'Bravissimo.' Standing ovation.
Why not . . . Oh, come in, Spring.

from

MIHI

English lesson

Acknowledgement to Bill Manhire

The naked family came into the room

The naked family comes into the room

The naked family has come into the room

The naked family will be coming into the room

*O Christ, what a mess: the naked family with halos
and donkey and all — and with a shitty-arsed baby
who needed wiping — is coming into the room again
from the patio.*

They would not of come into the room again

if my master, the Master Painter Giotto, had not of

let them in to sit for him — without the donkey.

Street scene from Olshausenstrasse Kiel, West Germany

Small pink and white flowers in pot-plants are being
  buzzed by green high-flying zebras.

The pot-plants are flanked by a pair of lanky-legged
  sunflowers, showing off — and beaming.

I can see them on the highest sub-alpine balcony
  opposite: there's a narrow walk-out to them

for the mobile watering can. The sunflowers are twin
  suns beaming a signal to me in duplicate.

The sunflowers fan the still air creating a small
  hurricane. Why, they're conducting a symphony

orchestra of lime trees responding to them from
  below; bowing, scraping — and clashing gummy

green leaves together, I think, tinnily, I can't
  read the score from here. Must be in German.

Visually, all the movements are just so full of glitter.
  It's too intensively rural — and urbanised — for

Wagner. The sunflowers take another bow. Separately.
  I reach for a pen: my hand nudges a bottle.

Toroa: albatross

Day and night endlessly you have flown effortless of wing
    over chest-expanding oceans far from land.
    Do you switch on an automatic pilot, close your eyes
    in sleep, Toroa?

On your way to your home-ground at Otakou Heads
    you tried to rest briefly on the Wai-o-te-mata
    but were shot at by ignorant people.
    Crippled, you found a resting-place at Whanga-nui-a-Tara;
    found space at last to recompose yourself. And now

    without skin and flesh to hold you together
    the division of your aerodynamic parts lies whitening
    licked clean by sun and air and water. Children will
    discover narrow corridors of airiness between, the suddenness
    of bulk. Naked, laugh in the gush and ripple — the play
    of light on water.

You are not alone, Toroa. A taniwha once tried to break out
    of the harbour for the open sea. He failed.
    He is lonely. From the top of the mountain nearby he calls
    to you: Haeremai, haeremai, welcome home, traveller.

Your head tilts, your eyes open to the world.

This poem was written for Wellington sculptor Tanya Ashken. A 'telephoned'
version was submitted to the Wellington Sculpture Trust from Dunedin, and
published by them on 19 May 1986 to coincide with a simple 'handing over'
ceremony of Tanya's work to the City of Wellington.
    A historical footnote was provided by Steve O'Regan and the poem was
read by Ray Henwood, actor.

Für mich der Vogel schön singt

It's no owl's cry or bittern that I can be precise about:
amiable company through the long hours.
What sweet bird is this then, singing in the night?
And through what grey hours silvered in song?

In my birthland there are no night-songs sung more
cheerfully than you sing, bird. Physically you are very
close. Your voice enfolds me.
I'm a poor mimic, but when I latch on to your key, we
manage a musical phrase together.

I have a defecting left ear which disorientates me.
For a whole week now I've opened and shut
cupboard and wardrobe doors, fearful
that I had slammed a door inadvertently on your day-time
resting-place. But as the long twilight thickens, your
voice in perfect German greets me:
Guten Abend, Herr Dichter: Guten Abend

You are bird of good omen. From my country good news
from Michael has stretched a warm hand to touch me
in this new house on: Old Houses Street, in this busy canal
city on the Baltic.

I'm not quite alone: you're here.
But Margret is gone. Death has finally taken
her father firmly by the hand. I hope to hear from her
again soon. Verily, on heaven and hell alike the sun shines.
How I wish she were here now, bird — to identify you; share
your message of solace; hint of joy.

Weekend in a
South Island city

The stars were
clear blood-pumping
eyeballs of light
he remembered: but

that was the night
before the night
it snowed.

No raised cheer
for that morning
when it came blear
one-eyed,
snow-encrusted.

The tight hills looking
like Boston (Sally) buns:
orange and blue-black
currants for houses set in
around the edges.

Everything unreal
different: like a womb
with central heating

We, who live in darkness

It had been a long long time of it
wriggling and squirming in the swamp of night.
And what was time, anyway? Black intensities
of black on black on black feeding on itself?
Something immense? Immeasureless?

No more.
There just had to be a beginning somehow.
For on reaching the top of a slow rise suddenly
eyes I never knew I possessed were stung by it
forcing me to hide my face in the earth.

It was light, my brothers. Light.
A most beautiful sight infiltered past
the armpit hairs of the father. Why, I could
even see to count all the fingers of my hands
held out to it; see the stain — the clutch of
good earth on them.

But then he moved.
And darkness came down even more oppressively
it seemed and I drew back tense; angry.

Brothers, let us kill him — push him off.

This poem refers to the rebellion by the children of Rangi and Papa.

The kumara god smiles fatly

Thinner than a silver blade curving
the moon has stopped climbing.
It is turning to me slowly until
full-faced I see the deep pits and
the nicks it has given itself shaving
without water
without a water mirror.

It seems to hang up there inert;
influential.

I have felt the silver pulse beat
of the moon its sandpaper hands
on my head on my heart my naked body
sanding my eyeballs.
I don't want to look at it anymore.

Face down between long valleys
of meshed kumara vines the earth smells
of woman flesh just milked.

I am bathing in a river of silver.
I am bathing in a thousand refractions.
The river empties itself into the pits:
my river my tears of silver. The moon

is gone.
And gone forever are things magical
I may never reach out to touch again
as gentle.

At dawn
the kumara god smiles fatly.
The time of harvest does not eclipse
my regret.

Today I'm gonna cover everything

The sun has taken a sickie. I window-shop,
juggling and palming small change in my pockets;
nudging to check whether twin neighbours just
beyond the fabric are at home.
The fistful of small change is of no consequence.
I shall find a seat in the library out of the wind,
check to see if the unemployed are reading Marx.

For those bright and colourful commodities behind
the jeweller's shop windows require real
folding money from Bonn, Tokyo, London, Geneva
and Washington to purchase, anyway.

I walk on, pausing
to light a cigarette butt while I perve
the tailor's dummies (naked) out of the corners
of my eyes. They have that glazed look about them
I guess, with what might be called, the anonymous
look of the inanimate — the soul-destroying

art of the plasterers-of-paris, out-of-work sculptors?
Wrong. Here, the school of Expressionism has reached
its apogee. I mean, they really do have that far-out
lavender freshness of European niceness — a blow-wave
classic look of vacancy and light. Most of them
are anorexic females with skinny arms, legs and
bodies. In another setting, perhaps, fugitives from

Buchenwald — and possessed of such varieties
of sameness; inane ironies of expression.
I juggle my centimes and balls, defensively, I think,
simply to keep my hands warm. It's cold.
The male dummies aren't completely disrobed. I'm told
they lack genitalia of any sort. Well, that figures.
I flick my cigarette away.

I'm buoyed aloft by the thought
that only my balls have that special fragrance that is
of me-on-earth. Correction: *me-on-earth living*, that is
before I used the scented Pakeha soap on them.

Lunch-time.
I buy a paper, and head out for the pie-cart
at the station.

Traffic statistic

for Hone Whitau

That day out there, at Te Kai-hinaki, I saw the pines do a slow
    hula in the sun. The wind seemed relieved to discover a
    softer voice again in the high branches. Robed and
    impassive, the Church Apostles helped to draw things
    together for you.

Your people are not demonstrative, and didn't seem to want to
    say much to you as they lowered you back into the womb
    of Earth.
    Well, a physical parting is a desolate thing. It's so final.
    And when you died (hell, you didn't muck about) that
    dazzling damsel, Aniwa-niwa, didn't come out for a grand
    appearance until the storm had unclenched her fists.

Fantastic now to recall the thrown earth, gravelly and river
    smooth — like brush-strokes and thumps on a kettle-drum
    — lisping drily on your coffin lid. The sun pressed warmly
    down on people in their good clothes, and the boats at
    anchor at Moeraki wiggled and chuckled and slopped.
    That day, Tangaroa, without hurry, withdrew his fingers
    . . . Last stop, anyway. You had come home.

Afterwards, in your house, we all got fat on good food and
    drink. The weight had lifted and you felt good for us. I
    know that. And I heard a clutch of piano-players play
    memory-songs on sweet ivories: black and white keys
    rippling. We sang. We danced.
    But somehow I kept thinking of your death and how
    wasteful it was. You think now: two cars charging
    headlong toward each other like bulls — and locking
    horns. The silence, Hone, can build just as mutely as a
    massive heap of nuts and bolts rusting in the rain.

In that kind of war, Hone, no one wins except the insurance
    companies. You are not conscripted. You don't have to
    wear a uniform. And I will say to you now, Hone, a poem
    is just as hard to build as a concrete bridge. But they both
    help people to get across . . .

The super powers rattle their sabres play deadly war games

In a sky devoid of colour, a huge bird wheels
    in slow circles. There's a buzzard up
    there turning . . . It's got zoom-lens
          for eyes.

In a leaden sky quite dead it moves, predatory
    claws retracted — but ready. Its
    droppings are not nourishment nor
    food for rose gardens; tree tomatoes.

One steel-encased turd generates an explosive
    force equal to 50,000,000 tons
    of T.N.T. Yup! and when the shit
    hits the fan — POW — ow — ow —
          ow.

    The buzzard is an American bird.

A brown bear lopes in and out of treeless, desert
    places, huge and cuddly. In far-out
    countries like totara-lands and kauri,
    frozen lands like Antarctica, breathless
    with innocence and vodka it goes.

In unnatural habitats, like Vietnam, it pretends
    to adapt itself, distributing Cuban cigars.
    Its progress is closely monitored by the
    buzzard. The bear yearns to embrace the
    World in a vice-like grip of steel. There's
    a missile site hidden up its arsehole.

    The bear is Russian.

Waiata tangi

E hiko ra, e . . .
Te uira i tai ra,
kapo-taratahi ana
te tara i Taramoe: ko te tohu
o te mate i nunumi ake nei

E tu, e Tiopira, i te ihu o te waka
Nga hae roroa
Te 'whatu taku, e 'Peta,
I maunu atu ai
te taniwha i te rua.

This poem is based on the first ten lines of a waiata tangi composed by Tamati
Hone, of the Ngati Ruahine tribe, for his children and tribes-people killed in
the attack on Sentry Hill Redoubt, Taranaki.

The Maori text for the waiata tangi was dictated by Te Whareaitu, of
Ngahau kainga, to James Cowan. In all, there are fifty-four typed lines, with
marginal notes by Cowan, which relate to place names and names of people
mentioned in the waiata tangi.

Students of oral and written Maori literature may consult the basic source
material and full text in Maori, in Folio No. M5, Manuscript Section, Alexander
Turnbull Library, Wellington, together with a literal translation submitted by
David Gregg, of Wellington, on 30 November 1977.

My poem, 'Lament', is intended solely to provoke interest in the work by
Tamati Hone. It is not a literal translation as such, but a salute to a fine poet,
and the Taranaki people in their struggles. I submit the first ten lines of Tamati
Hone's composition, 'Waiata tangi'.

Lament (2)

A random scrawl of lightning
  to the east is the jagged
  spear broken at Taramoe.

I saw you, Tiopira, take your
  place firmly and to the forepart
  of the canoe. Frail breath,
  alas, misting away, Hapeta.

From breast to knee-cap twin cuts
  long on myself inflict — THERE!
  And THERE! Aaha — haa!

Yes. Let it run.
  Grief is the monster uncoiling
  in the pit: blood-flow appease.

In the house that George and Dawn built

Neither erect nor supine, heavy-lidded and blear
    I look out through the dormer window of the upstairs
    room of your warm house.
    A dawn listless and drab provides enough far light
    to block in — here, there — the soft foliage of your
    kowhai tree, strong-stemmed, resilient; branching.

And now some kind of winged creature has found a secure
    foothold in it. I can't identify the dark-winged bird
    from its huddled silhouette. I refuse to accept that
    it is a dark and fateful omen, for the bird has opened
    its wings to give its armpits an airing and is shaking
    the night's dampness from them. It has completed other
    toilet requirements to begin the day. The noise
    of traffic builds, drowning out bird-chatter and gossip.

From a magnificent brass bed I rise, throwing my arms out and
    bringing them back with a kind of creakle. I work on this
    for a minute and then alter the direction by shooting my
    arms forward and bringing them back with more
    snap. Easy. *I mean, I've never read Jane Fonda.*

With my hands on my hips I roll my head around and around,
    listening to my unoiled neck-bones rattling; my ears
    popping. I work on that for a bit, and then with my feet
    wide apart, reach down again and again to touch my toes
    with my fingertips. My grunts are not a happy signal for
    success. Straightening up, I peer down over the curved
    horizon of my belly. I can just see my toes. There are
    ten of them. I'm pleased. My eyesight for that distance
    is quite exceptional. I think I'll live.

See what a little moonlight can do to you?

The moon is a gondola.
It has stopped rocking.
Yes. It's stopped now.

And to this high plateau
its stunning influence
on surge and loll of tides
within us should

somehow not go
unremarked
for want of breath
or oxygen.

And if I
to that magic micro-second
instant
involuntary arms reach out
to touch   detain

then surely
it is because you
are so good:
so very good to me.

Mad

W. M.

I'm too early.
I wait the long slow minutes out,
my breath inheld, ready
to balloon up into a high, but for the slow
exhalation of my excitement as you turn
into the magic avenue of trees — your hand
held out to me — your hand

to my multiple infarctions —
awarenesses
of coin-silver leaves turning a-squint in air,
muffled footfalls on the footpath;
your naked ankles twinkling in the autumn light.
I close the distance between us
as quickly

as fog does boiling in
from the inner harbour inexorably
as the thunder and beat of train wheels
flashing past a tiny country station just
standing there aghast and quite
inexplicably shaken and lost and
without say.

Well, that is how you infect me: mad ay?

Droll

Well, you know
    until you came, I was in a nowhere situation
    disembodied; of course, lost.

    And finding each other again, stretched out
    a hand reaching for the me of me just lying
    there quiescent and meek: a state

    known to everybody — I mean every body — as
    the helplessness of the tyrant flesh.
    A circumstance I can tell you, that was quite

    unforgettably forgettable, that is
    until you came.

Yes: and yes —
    pushed out a friendly hand you did devoid
    of wedding ring sapphire and suchlike glitter;
    wrist and ankle-bangles

    Smooth fingers firm, you took me in hand o
    and o o flesh-pulse prancing — thunder of hooves.
    There were small impediments, I must admit

    divesting all but our lapsed divinity — and may
    I add, virginity — my fingers like subversive slinks
    oiling against each other:

    nefarious art-thieves they.

My rooms are on the second floor of a two-storeyed building
    made of bricks: it is just a room with two windows
    a pushed-in ceiling, unwaxed floor

    and a flowered wall upon which no bees yearn
    to land, good only for wailing against, that is
    until you came.

Dear cousin

Some day soon old friend, before either
of us can throw our hand in, I'll say
to you: come.

Then, I'd roll out my threadbare whaariki
— to help you remember to take your boots
off — spread an old newspaper on the floor

and on it place a steaming pot of puha,
kamokamo, riwai, brisket-on-the-bone and
dumplings what we call: doughboys.

For sweeteners, I'll produce another pot
of boiled fish-heads with onions, cracking
open the heads afterwards for the succulent

eyes and the brains: that will be a special
treat, because we're both brainy buggers.
Then — because I know that you are also

a devout man — deeper than any prayer can
grab you — I will say simply: go for it.
And we'd crack a bottle or three together

you and me, swap lies and sing: happy days
are here again.
We would never hurt ourselves because we

wouldn't have far to bump our heads sitting
on the floor where only a small effort
is needed to roll over, rise on one knee

stand up — go out and wring your best friend's
neck. What do you reckon, cous?

Comedy of errors

From a distance
I saw the bird hopping
towards me in the rain
treating me as if I were
another worm or tree.
Wooden-faced

I stopped whirling my
umbrella but couldn't
control my eyeballs which
kept rolling down down
as the bird approached
glancing alertly from side
to side before coming
closer. I observed

that each time the bird
came to a halt it stood with
a sort of lean-on. It stopped
when I got it lined up with
the foresight on the bridge
of my nose. It had only

one leg on which to stand:
this being in line with a new
centre of gravity I suppose
and I began to curse the errant
stone which had sheared a leg
off the bird

but to my surprise
out of a bomb-bay of feathers
the bird lowered the other one
and I saw at once that the
unused leg was longer. When I
remarked to the bird that it
would have to use the long one
more the bird cocked its head
shone an eye at me and said:

you stupid worm I favour
this leg. It's my sore one.

171

from

SHORT BACK & SIDEWAYS

Bird of prayer

On the skyline
a hawk
languidly typing
a hunting poem
with its wings

Sun o (2)

Gissa smile Sun, giss yr best
good mawnin' one, fresh 'n cool like

yore still comin' — still
half in an' half outa the lan'scape?

An' wen yore clear of that eastern rim
of hills an' tha whole length of tha

valley begins to flood wit yr light, well
that's wen I could just reach out 'n stroke

tha pitted pock-marked pores of yr shiny
skin an' peel ya — just like a orange, right

down to yr white under-skin, but I wouldn't
bite ya — well, not until the lunch-bell goes

at noon wen I can feel ya hot an' outa reach
an' balanced right there — above my head.

C'mon, gissa smile Sun.

Well — I — never

Waist deep and crouched down by the pool-side
    the rocks looked solemn; there were five of them
    hid bald and tight-knuckled in reflective shadows.
    On the surface of the pool itself, a narrowing
    carpet of light pointing to the moon was laid on
    for us until it fractured when we got into it.
    For a while, it looked as if the moon was going
    to stay still, forever.

Well, just beyond this encircling haven we could hear
    the turbulence of water in the river gushing and
    very happy to lower its level below my chin just
    so I could keep my head above water. My body
    immersed, I can feel your exciting ballerina legs
    draped over my shoulders at the knees — heels
    threshing and in no way consigned to inaction like
    a flop-eared Dali watch — my mouth making a junction
    with your hair, your pubic mount of Eden.

Now as you gurgle your joy we drown in violent scrummage
    and squirm of bodies lassooed by a whirling cosmic
    string of sperm engraced by and enlacing the pearly
    gate. Well, for a moment everything is stopped.

When I shoot up again for air the pulsing cry of crickets
    telephoning each other seems to obtrude above all else
    except for the slide-fit of you bearing down as I stretch
    up up on my toes from the pool-bed/o, a real Space Dick/
    and counting only four dark sinewy rocks awash now
    in disturbed water, the other engulfed by your thighs —
    your legs hooked around my hips, my back, like a giant
    rosary as you begin chanting a mantra, a benediction, and
    pouring beads of sweet poison or something into my deaf
    ear and leaving me a-splutter . . . and o, breath-tooken.

Kitten

the phone didn't ring
yesterday.

it never even looked like
starting

and no letters've come
today, either — except

a stray kitten

i have given it milk;
it has adopted me

we've had a brief talk
about his mum? his dad?

you might say it was
a one-sided chat about cats:

but nothing's come of it

kitten knows only two
words and one of them is:

slurp

it is making love to my
feet: it understands

my loneliness . . . miaow?

Imp

(to Juliet)

Wind furrowed are
the sea pastures where
white horses prance
your eyes merry me
the corners of the
heart a mouth
uptilted

Tour bus minutiae, and commentary: West Berlin, 1985

I have felt the bite & crunch of winter winds, the sudden
stir of snow hunched around the corner waiting to pounce
on me. I'm envigoured by it. It's called: Berliner Luft:
Duft, Duft, dufte! Loverly.

Dog-lovers walk their pets home, anxious to complete
the chore quickly, a marvel of detachment & poise as the dog
pisses or shits. When new snow lies white on the ground,
the nature-mess that dogs make is easier to see and avoid.

There are over a hundred thousand dogs registered
in Berlin. The City Authorities are sympathetic.
Two hundred and fifty thousand trees have been planted.

Despite the generosity of statistics, there are canine
territorial disputes over the third tree. Tribal Elders
from my Dog Tribe — Ngati Kuri — will send a mediator
to Geneva, me. It's not a piddly matter.

Every tree has been given a number which I find phantastisch!
You may rendezvous with the beautiful Dame from East Berlin
unter den Linden tree Nummer 2231 Eisenberger Strasse.
On the Wannsee border-bridge, a Spy Exchange Service —
Spionageaustauschdienst — is in place.

Dead leaves, which carpet drain and pathway, are cleared away
by City Council workers who come from Italy and Türkei.
Five tons of dog-dung is collected every day.

Bottled bio-gas from such a rich source is exported.
Gas ovens at Dachau & Auschwitz have been made redundant.
A taped recording of mixed doggy-barks is enclosed with each
bottle. I'm not impressed . . . Doggy-bark recording is a dubious
practice.

On the Lietzensee Ufer the trees are stark and still. A ridge
of snow rests along the tops of their nobbly, snaky branches,
their dark winter bareness, fattened and enhanced. On the frozen
lake, voices go up in steam — to the hiss of skates, sluicing . . .

Inside the warm pub on Nachod Strasse a dog comes in wagging its owner, Sabine, on the end of a leash. Sabine orders a coffee, unwinds her scarf. The dog sits down by her feet. Helmut, a Berliner, greets her with tongue-in-cheek: 'Sabine, kommen Sie hier bei Fuss?'

Dear Brown Bear City, I love you. Ach ja! You're a bloody wonderful ache.

NEW POEMS

Dour note on a sunny winter's morning

to J.L.

I am unacquainted with the World's
sadnesses, knowing only
its specificities and the pain
of separation — the aftermath
of joyful couplings that were
unproclaimed — of births that are

unadvertised,

and a million more looking like
death with never a listing on tomb
or tabloid, obelisk.

They go unremarked except in the vague
and pretty language of poetry — with
its pitiless ironies, ambiguities
openness and love.

Who are the real infidels?

Sitting on your horse out there, rock-steady,
    pathetically alone, you're confronted by row
    upon row upon row of horsemen swords drawn
    and held upright between the eyes; their eyes
    aglitter with the passion of it; horses impatiently
    pawing the ground. Horse and sword steadied by wrists
    of iron — nerves tightened, attendant on your command.

And you, the seemliest
    of all your burnoosed cousins
    are as imperturbable as stone standing on four legs.
    And as you bark a warning, sword-points flash downward
    insinuating themselves into the outer lips of scabbards
    teasingly, but no further . . . And now

    as you turn your horse side-on to your men, you face
    the women arranged like black shelves; row upon row
    upon receding row against the hills watching silently;
    their black dresses pressed against their bodies by a
    wind flappably distraught.

You draw your sword
    and kissing it, salute them. The hills stir, come alive
    with the murmur and growth of sound and movement, and
    wheeling again to face your battalions, your shouted
    command of only three words — short, incisive, cutting
    the air like whip-cracks: LET US GO!

And oho for the hisses, the sibilances
    of three thousand swords scabbarded — joining as one
    with the tremulous cries, the yodelling gurgle and sigh
    of the women — there's hurt and pride in it — for the
    warriors who may never return.

Wheeling, you give your sword-point direction. Your horse walks;
sedately; as if there were time; and three lines form behind
you until you're but a speck in the distance and the proud
high stepping trot begins: the women-cries swell as the
rhythm grows into a canter — a canter that does not weary
but devours distances and the enemy who come dashingly
to meet their doom with the resigned elegance of the damned
(or the very stoned) — and whose only Pledge is:

We die gladly now for the United States: for the only HELL
that's left, is . . . Y E-E-E-E S! (goddammit)

When words were coded and replaced by numbers

9

see — iron driven into my feet, my hands — hold
me aloft defying the gravity of it

8

and long after the white ball ballooned
and the predictable rain fell there
were just no more questions left to
ask nor easy answers black and white
left or right — just more wrong ones
either/or, for or against — and only a
handful queuing just a mite too late to see
me rise like the yeast of the bread I Am:

anyway

7

all the world's people now are blended
a pot-pourri of blooms long gone long
dead, up-ended:

6

intriguingly
and balanced thinly on thin air
a whiff of perfume, man-made
heaven-scent: amen

5 4 3 2 1

0

Frau Maria Wischhausen

Involuntarily, in slow motion
    are the movements shaping your stillness —

    your stillness; that austere thing
    the static lines of which might only
    be memorialised briefly in action.

Incuriously and without haste
    you follow the arcing edge and flow
    of your conversational flood, and that
    which is unspoken — and not in English:

    that which is the still centre
    of your ease — as the noonday valleys
    of your childhood in Österreich lay
    at ease — dream-a-slack but unslaked
    in the dream-stream shimmer
    of a felled day — wishing now to step

    outside the Altar of your altered self
    sauna-whipped, crackling — your newness
    an oscillation of the senses — tiny
    barely definable gestures to out-gesture
    the helpless unauthorised retreat
    to that inner sanctum into which I shall
    not place a foot nor burgle.

And to the memory — that ancestor of fear
    and pain, joy and exaltation, shame
    and pleasure: a private act of will;
    self-lured, alluring.

He pao reka mo Huaonia

Aa, whaka-mahiatia atu oku ringa-ringa kia paa
    atu. Aa, ka paa. Aa, ka mahi.
    Kia mohio koe, penei tonu ano te ahuatanga o nga
    ringa mo te nanao tuna, mo te tiwara-wara kutai
    e taku Tau. Aa, ka timata ahau ki runga, ki nga
    huru-huru papai o to matenga — Aue! Te kanapanapa —
    te roroa hoki. Maku e pangaa atu ki muri kia watea
    ai o taringa, to kakii.

Ka taku arero anake e kihia e horoi — e mitia atu
    i te hiriwa me te koura o ta taua hia-hia-tanga.
    Ehoa! Kaua e pouri. Kua tae atu oku ngutu
    ngote-ngote whakareka atu ana i o Uu . . . mmm —
    Kaua koe e tangi mai rite tonu i te Raapeti.

A taea te pehea. E tangi mai ana koe? Ha! mo te aha?
    Ko te reka o te hari? 'Kii mai ana koe me hurry-hurry up?
    Aianei, ka tino niho-tia atu koe kia mohio koe i te
    kino o te mamae! Whaaki mai i to hia-hia —

Naa . . . kua tae taku arero ki to pito — mitimitia atu.
    A, kua heke oku ringaringa ki raro, tutuu mai ana —
    whawha-tia atu ana to ngahere, a, kua kitea!
    Kua kitea nga momona-tanga o to ngahere, o kukupa
    hoki e ngu ngu mai ana, a, kua rere mai ano
    te hinu — he hinu tou-tou taro, kumara, aha ranei,
    kia reka rawa atu te maa-ene-ene o te heke iroto
    i te korokoro.

Kore e whaaki mai ki 'au te tikanga o ta raua rapunga.
    Heoi nei, a mahi ana i ta raua mahi i raro mai i nga
    huruhuru o taua maunga. He toa kaitiaki hoki ki tua atu
    i nga ngutu o tau ano kuaha, tatari mai ana — puukana
    mai ana! Whaka-piko atu taku tuara: maatakitaki . . .

Engari, kua ara mai ano tetahi toa maia — uaua; hiakai!
    Poua atu he taki — au, au, auee — ha! Huri-ku-a-oro mai
    nga whetu katoa o te Ao.

Frances, baby . . .

I talk with you and you
track my voice back
with a tiny finger I
unhook from my lower lip.

I hold a candle to your
eyes passing it from side
to side. You look past it
to something else, beyond.

You don't notice me until
I light the candle.
The candle guts out almost
drowning until

it begins to glow inside
your eyes inviting me in.
I snuggle down level
seeing eye to eye

with you at last. But
you are not he: nor are
you me holding a candle
irradiating us.

But you are him. And I
am content. I blow out
the candle and it wicks
out smelling strongly

of smoke. I put it aside
blending into your darkness
your softness kissing you
and we're folded together

in love and darkness forever.
Yet I'm so unutterably lost
my yearnings deepen:
I light the candle again

I try to be smart alec and
alert to your secret babblings
upsetting you hugely
when I get it all wrong.

Poem for Marilynn Webb: Gore, 1986

You introduce me to a bright-eyed young man who must be quite
    the youngest Gallery Director in New Zealand.
    Wine? I shake my head. The Gallery is new.

    With a can of beer in my hand, but unencumbered by a Programme
    listing your numbered prints, I take a quick cruise around
    the Gallery. Well, people who do that are either showing off
    or just plain broke. For I have the feeling

    the Critics, the mafia-men of art, the parochial manipulators,
    buzz the City Galleries like hairy meteors unencumbered by
    a Programme, but like Royalty, are the first to leave without
    meeting the artist who might be from the wop-wops, Tutae Kuri
    River, or worse — a woman.

But what a feed. I've never seen so much of you in one go.
    I move more slowly around the Gallery a second time, edging
    past immobile groups of people sipping wine and chatting.
    I have a problem with red and green when they're meshed-in
    with other colours. To concentrate, I pause in front of number
    eighteen making a tunnel of my fist to look through. Your
    colours leap out to hongi me. Your rune-like letters

    are your personal code-marks on stone, or, incised in pottery.
    Your rainbows aniwa-niwa themselves out of nowhere and into
    your lake prints with a smoky splash. Lake fish of immense size
    leap out of Lake Mahine-rangi to catch a ride on your rainbow-
    escalator, and in a great migratory arc drop into Lake Taupo
    in the North Island, thinner; much paler. It's the new
    Maori/Celtic Legend.

Lover, mother, daughter of sun and air, Earth & Sky, your woman's
    hands speak for us all; unaggressive, yet protective, they
    are as soft and open as the faces of small children.
    But the faces of the grubby, greedy little men who wish to
    pollute the earth and blow it up, just haven't been leaned on
    heavily enough yet. They're being identified: by a steam-roller.
    I make this prophecy: before the sterile ugliness of chemicals
    and bombs — your caring hands shall endure. Sonorous words?
    Not at all. Blake would share a mead-bowl with you. And Turner.
    I'd bring a half gallon of it too, if you'd cook a memorable
    crab chowder. Yr own. Not Aunt Daisy's.

Well, standing beside you at last, I reach across your shoulders
pulling you close to me. Hip-locked for a moment, I mutter
something monosyllabic like: yeah, good — hoping I don't sound
unctuous — anxious, even. Arrested, my eyes have been taken
into custody. Arraigned before your colour Bar of inventive in-
cursions into new dimensions — of looking, of feeling — without
demur, my eyes have accepted their sentence: it's for life.

Deep river talk

It's cold: it's golden; a magnificent
orange disc playing peek-a-boo
from the far-side of straggly
strings of leafless rastafarian willows
growing on the other side of the river.
The river's wide here: it's

undecided: it's steeling itself
never to turn and go back uphill.
Steam's rising from it and it's
not the early morning sun that's
doin' it; I can't raise heat
from the sun yet.

The veins of the river are swollen.
They're bending to the tide's
up-swing: tempers are like sails
shredding in a gale.

There's talk of a merger. A know-all
insect on stilts has just walked out
on top of the waters to supervise
the talks; I suppose pretending
to be Jesus.

In the sunlight mullet are jumpin'
and making lovin' archways of silver
for the migratory ocean-seeking eels
eeling their way down down; down
to the river-mouth and away.

The river's pushy, 'Back off! Thus far
and NO further —'

'I'll see YOU outside, mate,' says
the sea, turning. A swish, a tiny
whip and swirl of water —

Snap!

Daddy-long-legs has joined his
ancestors by way of a hungry trout's
stomach & stomach-ejector.

Happens to people too, nowadays — with
sharks hangin' around a lot.

... *the sea chanting lugubriously*
the rain patting me for hidden weapons

for Carol & Greg & Doreen of Balclutha

people who walk around in the rain naked
don't get wet: they get washed

and people who are not allergic to wearing
woollens silks nylon & cotton things next
to their skins think they're being picked on
when they get drenched and wet through RUNNING
in the rain pausing only to pull
their dark glasses on & pretending not
to look at the naked ones WALKING
in the rain without a care
or stitch on

the few who rub insect repellent on in bright sunshine
who walk the beach naked at noon don't get any weta
than people who wrap dark glasses around
themselves for protection from the fierce sun
only to take them off quickly
to watch the naked ones paying homage to tangaroa
as they bend down to scoop up a wavelet or two to kiss
making everyone — just everybody
purse their lips as well

but today's different: god's got such a huge
bladder: he's so . . . so relentlessly up there — and
using newton's law on everyone to get even yeah and biffing
apples down on us as well: for christ's sake y'know?

rain today — and rain again tomorrow — the sea
chanting lugubriously: and I'm thinkin' well

forever's a nice change naked — till my clothes dry
on the line anyway before all the dye runs out:
's like being born anew only hairier

Index